STRONGER TOGETHER

STRONGER TOGETHER

STEPHANIE YUEN

NEW DEGREE PRESS

COPYRIGHT © 2021 STEPHANIE YUEN

STRONGER TOGETHER

ISBN   978-1-63730-836-3   *Paperback*

             978-1-63730-900-1   *Kindle Ebook*

             978-1-63730-951-3   *Ebook*

Dedication

To My Loving Family: Mom, Dad, Tiffany, who constantly support me no matter what.

To my friends and family who are always there at a moment's notice and motivate me to be my best and most genuine self.

CONTENTS

PART ONE

INTRODUCTION

———

After a humid May school day during my seventh-grade year in 2014, I came home, yelled, "Hey, Mom!" and ran upstairs to take a shower. It was a day like any other, but when I looked down this time, I noticed clumps of my hair surrounding me in the bathtub.

At that time, I wasn't too worried. I formulated plenty of excuses in my head. It was probably due to having my hair pulled back too much or having it too tight. I thought nothing of it and did not tell my parents. For the next week or so, I let my hair down and did not tie it up once. However, one night, as I was doing my homework and getting stuck on a math problem (as usual), I ran my right hand through my hair as I got more and more frustrated. Suddenly, I felt little, prickly things on my scalp. It turned out to be baby hairs; the texture was like a man's stubby moustache. Again, I thought nothing of it, so I didn't bother going to the mirror to check.

Then came the next day. As I washed my hair, the same thing happened. As I rubbed shampoo and conditioner in my hair and rinsed it out, clumps of my hair accumulated in my hand. I hurriedly finished showering and checked my scalp in the mirror. Lo and behold, I found a dime-shaped bald spot. It stuck out like a sore thumb. I stared at it for about ten minutes. I was so scared to tell my parents. What if I did something to make my hair fall out like that?

I finally built up the courage to show my parents my bald spot and they were immediately panicked. For the next few months, my mom helped me wash my hair.

I will never forget hearing my mother quietly sob as she washed and brushed my hair. She didn't want me to hear. She tried to hide the crying, but despite her best efforts, I could still hear the quietest sniffles. She was equally as frightened as I was. We didn't know what was happening. Frankly, we were scared shitless.

I was thirteen years old at the time, amidst puberty—the awkward stage of life everyone experiences. I kept the news strictly within my family. It started out as a bald spot, yet it quickly progressed and I lost more than 80 percent of my hair. After dealing with the spots for two months, I made the decision to shave it off and finally free myself from the person I didn't like seeing in the mirror. Neither my parents nor my family know this, but I would take a towel and cover the mirror so I would not have to see my reflection when I brushed my teeth. Seeing my hair fall out right before my eyes, more and more every day, made me upset and scared.

It was only two months after receiving the diagnosis my alopecia areata, or just patchy hair loss, rapidly progressed to alopecia universalis, or hair loss of my entire body. During that process, I had alopecia totalis, or total hair loss of my scalp, before losing all the hair on my body. Some individuals may only lose the hair on their head or have bald patches on their scalp. Others, like me, may have complete hair loss. As mentioned, I started off with alopecia areata. The hair loss got to a point where I only had a couple of strands on my head. So, I decided to do the deed and shave off the rest of the random spots. I felt *liberated* when I shaved off the rest of my hair. My dad, on the other hand, teared up. It was definitely difficult; I felt as if I was losing a part of me. Now, I know it's "just" hair, but hair is a way women express themselves. I am blessed to be healthy and loved by so many people, yet when I see other girls walking on campus or sitting in class playing with their hair or styling it in some way, it makes me upset sometimes. The decision to shave off the rest of my hair was only a week before I started the eighth grade—not the brightest decision since I cried almost every night leading up to the first day of school. I was terrified, lonely, and clueless.

I was so lucky to have a teacher in my middle school, Ms. Chandler, who had alopecia as well. She reached out to me one day and had such an impact on my journey. In times of frustration, she was the person I could turn to and ask questions. When my hair first fell out, I did not know what was going on. I didn't know if there was something wrong with me that was causing this change. Ms. Chandler's kindness and expertise were such a huge turning point for me that a few words in a book wouldn't do her justice. She really has been supportive in shaping me; without her, I would not be the positive person I am today. The day I took control was the day I shaved my hair, but that does not mean I immediately gained 100 percent confidence as the last bit of hair was shaved off.

I didn't even have the courage to tell my best friends. I was so scared they would view me differently when they saw me without hair. I was also hesitant and extremely self-conscious about my wardrobe because from experience, many individuals thought I was a boy since I did not have any hair, wore no makeup, and was usually wearing a sweatshirt. I had many encounters with individuals who called me "sir" or thought I was a boy for a while.

The summer of 2019, I was accepted to be a youth mentor for the National Alopecia Areata Foundation, or NAAF for short. By July of 2019, I had my first mentee request for me to be her mentor. It was extremely rewarding. She was struggling with doing her makeup and feeling comfortable in her own skin when she would go out in public. I have been able to give her makeup tutorials to help, such as what products I use to do my eyebrows and eyeliner and how to apply them. We text regularly and communicate via other forms of social media. I am there to offer advice and encouragement on her low days. I was in the same position she was when I first lost my hair. It's all new. No one in our families understood what we were going through. It's a very challenging experience and I'm glad I was able to help her just as Ms. Chandler had done for me.

Losing hair at thirteen years old during puberty—when everything about you personally, emotionally, and physically is changing—is hard. I would have crying episodes and my parents were sometimes frustrated or annoyed. Maybe it was because they were frustrated with themselves since they did not know how to help me cope. My mentee goes through similar emotions and I am able to help her since I understand. When she has any question or concern, I am the person she can ask and confide in, and I take so much pride in that. It makes me so happy to help others and make a difference in their lives, whether it be big or small.

That's just the *CliffsNotes* of my journey that took me from a frightened middle schooler to activist. But before I go any further with that part of the story, let's talk about its backdrop: alopecia and societal norms.

According to the National Alopecia Areata Foundation, 147 million individuals worldwide have alopecia, yet many people do not have any knowledge about this condition, let alone have ever heard of it. If you saw a bald girl or woman at your local grocery store or mall, would you be like, "*Oh yeah, she has alopecia!*" or "*Oh no! Does she have cancer?*" Kudos to you if you picked option one; however, I typically get the she-has-cancer stares from people wherever I go. You know—the worried eyebrows, the big eyes, and the little frown. Sometimes, I do get approached and am asked if I have cancer, and I reply I have alopecia and have that chance to explain the condition to them. Nonetheless, for all the other times, people look at me while cupping their hands over their mouth to the ear of the person standing next to them.

That's a problem I explore in this book. People should not assume anything about anybody—especially in my situation; not all bald women are sick. Numerous females who have alopecia, both young and old, are afraid to speak about this condition because society has engraved these norms in our heads, like how long hair is beautiful and put on a pedestal. That's just not the case. I am fortunate to have such a strong support system, and I have not been bullied to the extent other alopecians have been. Because of the people around me who never treated me any differently because of my alopecia, I'm able to embrace my baldness and confidently speak about this condition and my journey.

I hope this book resonates with those with or without alopecia and provides a deeper understanding not just of people with alopecia, but of all people who are physically different and feel they need to hide some aspect of themselves in order to conform to society's standards. Through this book, I hope individuals get more than a glimpse of my life with alopecia—both the good and bad aspects. Through my story and many others', I hope this book can make fellow alopecians more comfortable in their own skin. I want to be that voice for others, and I hope I can achieve that. I want to make a difference in people's lives, whether it's big or small. I want to spread awareness about alopecia and dismantle the beauty standards set for bald women by society. I know it's a phrase that might be overused, but I hope people don't judge a book by its cover and get to know someone's personality before assuming anything based on physical appearance alone.

I want to be the person who can help, guide, and be there for people through their journeys just like many individuals were for me. I am a youth mentor for the National Alopecia Areata Foundation (NAAF) and a speaker for the Children's Alopecia Project (CAP). Being able to be there for others with the same condition brings me an abundance of happiness. Helping others is one of the reasons I am going to school in hopes of becoming a nurse in the near future. I hope to be able to work and thrive in an environment where everyone is able to be themselves and accepted and loved for that.

So, I hope your takeaway is this: Everyone is beautiful. From the hardships and trials we encounter along our journeys, we can always come out stronger. Regardless of whether you have alopecia or not, ignore the haters and the negative energy, and always be true to yourself. Be *you*.

1

THE DISCOVERY

———

It was an otherwise ordinary Tuesday night during my seventh-grade school year when I first noticed a bald spot on my head. My parents began to frantically search the Internet for answers, thinking it could be cancer-related. The next day, they insisted I still go to school and we would ride it out and see what happened. Like I said before, my parents insisted that I tied my hair too tight, so they told me to go to school with my hair down for the time being. We were all hoping the hair would just grow back. Everyone is familiar with the traditional storyline of bad guys attacking good guys. We see it everywhere in movies or television series; sometimes the plot twist has us learning a supposed "good guy" is only posing as a good guy when in reality they are working for the bad guys. Alopecia occurs when the good guy—in this case, the body's immune system—attacks its hair follicles, causing hair loss. In a sort of ironic twist, my body's good guys didn't seem to recognize my hair follicles as other good guys anymore. So, on an otherwise ordinary Tuesday night in May of my seventh-grade school year, my personal good guys vs. bad guys battle started unfolding.

Even when I wasn't washing it, my hair was falling out. As I brushed it or ran my hand through it, multiple strands of hair would flow between my fingers and fall to the floor. Since my parents and I decided to wait a little and see if it would grow back, going to school posed a new set of challenges. I would subconsciously run my hand through my hair throughout the day and when the period ended, I would see strands of my hair around my desk and chair. I hoped every day no one saw it. I would even use my shoes to spread the hair around so it wouldn't be centered around my area.

I didn't want my peers to see me picking up strands of hair from the floor and putting it in the trash and think it was weird. I would be so embarrassed. My thought process was everyone's hair sheds, so I could play it off as "everyone's hair," right? Wrong. I grew up in a predominantly white community, so the long strands of black hair couldn't belong to blonde-haired Nicole. As the days went on, my hair loss journey grew worse and patches of bald spots were visible. My parents bought this black fiber product that was a powder-like substance I could sprinkle on my bald spots so it would cover them up and blend into my scalp. Again, absentmindedly, I would run my hand through my hair and with a quick jolt back to reality, recognize what I had done and be so scared I had messed up the fiber.

I would run my hand through my scalp several times in a period and ask my teacher almost every time if I could use the bathroom. My teacher and classmates probably thought I had terrible IBS. I had that sweaty kind of anxiety at the mere thought of people noticing me get up so frequently to leave the classroom, terrified they'd stare at the back of my head and catch a glimpse of a bald spot. I power-walked out of the classroom like the elderly women you see speed-walking at the mall for exercise. It gave my classmates less time to stare at me. They probably didn't even care about me getting up, and I was just over-worrying and overthinking the whole situation. But on the inside, I was freaking out and longed for the glorious ring of the last bell for the school day so I could hop on a bus and head home.

After concluding my hair situation was only going to worsen, my parents took me to my pediatrician and she referred me to another doctor to take a biopsy of my scalp. Soon after, we went to the specialized doctor and he scraped a piece of my scalp and sent it into testing. We waited for the results for about a week. It felt like forever. I would run to the mailbox each day after school to check the mail. Yes, the results were sent by mail. I know, way back when. Finally, after the agony of waiting, we received the diagnosis: *Alopecia*.

Initially, I had no feelings of sadness or shock because, to be honest, I had no clue what alopecia was. At least my family and I had a sense of closure. Having a diagnosis helped us know what my condition was and we had a basis to start our research and learning process. I could research alopecia and all the facts, statistics, and treatments associated with it.

After conducting my initial research, I found out alopecia is an autoimmune disease that causes one's hair to fall out. Some are "lucky" and have their hair grow back again. The reason I put "lucky" in quotes is because I consider myself lucky. Although my hair has not grown back, I have met amazing people along the way. I became educated about this disease and more aware about how people around me might be experiencing different situations. You never know how someone is feeling or what a person is going through unless you experience a day in their shoes. Alopecia has also helped me form *quality* relationships with *quality* people.

They didn't care or seem to notice I didn't have hair. They saw past that, and I'm so lucky to have those people in my life. Let us backtrack a bit to the diagnosis again. Like I said, I had no clue what alopecia was. It did not run in my family and I did not know anyone who had the same condition. After looking it up on Google, I found there are various types of alopecia. The most common three are alopecia areata, alopecia totalis, and alopecia universalis.

Alopecia areata is hair loss formed in patches, alopecia totalis is where individuals lose all the hair on their head, and alopecia universalis is hair loss of the entire body with the exception of some places (National Alopecia Areata Foundation, 2020). For instance, I have alopecia universalis, but I have toe hairs (weird, right?). I don't have any hair on my head, eyebrows, eyelashes, arms, armpits, pubic area, or—wait for it—*legs!* Yes, you read that right. No leg hair. I haven't shaved my legs in seven years. It really has saved me a lot of time.

Others may have an ophiasis pattern, a subtype of alopecia areata that presents as a "symmetric, band-like pattern of hair loss on the occipital, temporal, and parietal regions of the scalp" (Asad et al., 2020). In other words, ophiasis-pattern alopecia is like reverse male-pattern baldness. To clarify, male-pattern baldness is when the hair is lost from the top/crown area down; however, for ophiasis-pattern baldness, it's when the hair is lost from the bottom up on the scalp.

Alopecia can come and go, or it can be permanent at any age. I know individuals who had alopecia their whole adolescent life but had hair regrow right before their wedding and then fall out again. Others may have it since birth. Both men and women may also have androgenic alopecia, which is the occurrence of hair loss at the top and front of the head for men and at the top and crown of the head for women. For me, my hair has regrown a couple of times (with help from prescribed medication or acupuncture and natural remedies), but not to the extent of a whole head of hair.

Alopecia affects people of both sexes and all ethnic groups. "In the US, approximately 6.8 million people are diagnosed with alopecia. It is said genetics play a role when it comes to this condition. It is a polygenic disease, which requires a contribution of genes that are inherited from both parents" (National Alopecia Areata Foundation, 2020). It is also said there is some sort of correlation between stress and hair loss. Currently, no cure exists for this disease; however, many have tried various treatments, whether they be natural home remedies, going to seek advice/treatment plans from a dermatologist, or even changing their diet.

At the time, my parents and I were introduced to various treatments or remedies. For the first couple of years after discovering I had alopecia, my frantic parents were in search of a Chinese doctor who could perform acupuncture or "massages" that would reverse the hair loss. We then were introduced to Dr. Wang, a friend of my grandparents who specialized in acupuncture treatment. My body did respond well to the acupuncture treatment. As the treatment progressed, I almost had a full head of hair. However, we decided to discontinue the treatment since my dad hadg to drive approximately three hours round trip every Tuesday and Thursday each week after a full workday. He would drive an hour to work, complete an eight-hour workday, come back home to pick up my mom, sister, and me, and then embark on another hour-and-a-half drive to the acupuncture location. We would spend an hour or so there and then take an hour and a half back. Plus, we thought it was "done" because I had already regained a full head of hair. But as soon as I stopped the treatment, all my hair fell out again.

Man, did that suck. Not only did we spend the time and effort going to see an acupuncturist, but I had to repeat the process of losing my hair. We thought it had worked, my hair was going to continue growing back, and I was "cured." I went through the same rollercoaster of emotions. This time, I was somewhat stronger. I was better equipped to not let the situation affect me too hard. Nevertheless, it was still difficult to go through again. At the vulnerable age of thirteen to fourteen years old, having to go through the hair loss process *twice* was a big smack in the face.

Every time I would sit at the dinner table, my parents, especially my dad, would come around and turn on his phone flashlight and check my head to see if there was any growth. Anytime he noticed a small, stubby black hair on my scalp, he would get excited and say it would grow back. But to be honest, it was tiring to keep a smile on my face. I did not know if my hair was going to grow back. And what if it did? Would it just fall back out again? I did not want it to give my parents any false hope. Every time they would become hopeful, it would make me more upset because I always asked why it was so important my hair was growing out. Was I not pretty without hair? Though it was not their intention, it made me feel hair was the sole defining factor of beauty.

Aside from doctor and acupuncture appointments, I have also tried following a strict regimen and eating foods that were listed on the diet index by Hairloss Protocol. The diet plan included various meal options that contained folate, vitamins D and A, and calcium. Meals had balanced sources of protein and vegetables, but they were all bland with little flavor, and I did not like following this regimen day after day. My hair did grow after a few months on this plan; however, the results were not consistent. I would have some regrowth, but it would fall out again even though I was sticking to the regimen. Therefore, I gave up on it. Seeing some regrowth would raise my hopes as well as my parents'. It was just a continuous cycle of hope and disappointment. Plus, I needed junk food; I was thirteen and tweenagers lived on junk food and sugary snacks.

After I gave up on home remedies and treatments, my physician recommended I see a doctor at the Children's Hospital of Philadelphia, commonly referred to as CHOP.

CHOP had a six-month waiting list. Gosh darn it. We scheduled it in August, and February seemed so far away. In the meantime, I was anxiously going to school and just trying to survive eighth grade.

It's Christmas 2014 right now, just two more months to go before the appointment. My family and I are heading to our church's Christmas Eve service. I dreaded wearing wigs and opted for a hat. However, I received a big, fat *no* from my mother. I didn't understand why, but I was not going to argue with my mother, especially on Christmas Eve. I reluctantly put on a short, black-colored wig and headed out the door. The wig resembled 2013 Rihanna's bob cut hairstyle; however, she rocked it and I wasn't feeling it. While sitting in the church pew, I just couldn't wrap my head around why I was not allowed to go to church without a wig. I paid no attention to the sermon while anger festered inside me. As I thought more about it, I asked myself if it was because my mom was embarrassed to have a bald daughter. I had no clue why and it created reasons in my head that made me feel terrible inside. Christmas is supposed to be a happy holiday where people celebrate with others, yet I was enraged, hurt, and still not fully comprehending the "why" surrounding the whole wig discussion. I tried to smile when I saw other people, but internally, I wanted to be anywhere else. With a blink of an eye, New Year's passed and it was February—time for my appointment.

My parents and I hopped in the car and headed to CHOP. Once we arrived and filled out the paperwork, we were taken into a room and the doctor ran tests and checked for swollen thyroids, lymph nodes, and other vital areas for signs that might signify something else other than alopecia. They didn't find anything else that would be alarming and confirmed it was indeed alopecia. I was then transferred to the dermatology department to discuss with a dermatologist any possible treatments that can aid in hair regrowth.

I've had biannual appointments at CHOP with Dr. Leslie Castelo-Soccio, a pediatric dermatologist who specializes in alopecia, since 2014. She offered to share some words about her expertise:

"I often see families struggle with the diagnosis of alopecia areata at first. The diagnosis is often sudden and unexpected and parents often feel a lot of worry about their child's future. They experience a unique type of grief. What I find humbling, though, as I follow their journey is the incredible resilience of children and their families as they decide their path for treatment or no treatment. I see amazing kids grow in knowledge and confidence with their alopecia."

Dr. Castelo has made such an impact on my life. She never makes me feel the need to take the treatments offered. I know it might be her job to do that; however, she makes me feel comfortable and she helps me realize sometimes the risks are not worth the reward. She never insists I go through certain treatments and leaves it to my discretion. For instance, some of the treatments have side effects that result in various types of cancer down the road. I am not willing to go through with those treatments if they present side effects that are detrimental to my health. I don't have hair. That's it. I'm healthy and I do not want to risk my health just for hair.

Many alopecians would explore various treatments and go through with them despite the possible side effects because they wanted their hair to grow back. Hair is a huge part of someone's identity, so maybe they go through with the treatment because they want to feel whole again. Some women may feel the need to go through with these treatments if they need to grow their hair to feel confident again. Society has correlated being bald with sickness and that just isn't the case. Bald people are beautiful and handsome and should not be told otherwise.

Hair loss can negatively affect someone's mental and physical health. It is difficult to see something that was once a part of you gone. Losing your hair at any age is not easy, but the decision to embrace the look? That's a whole other story. That's a story of overcoming challenges, a story of learning how to love yourself, and a story of grit. Throughout the rest of this story, I share my struggles and the struggles of others, and you will watch as I grow into the person I am today. Brace yourself!

PART TWO

2

THE DECISION

———

During that summer, I spent hours crying in my room and was terrified to go out in public. I would constantly question God, "*Why me? Why did I have to lose my hair?*"

I know the answer to that question now. It took me a few years, but I finally understand why I was given this *gift*. Alopecia took me on a rollercoaster of emotions and I viewed it as a curse during the beginning of my journey, constantly asking, *Why me?* I now view alopecia as a blessing. Without alopecia, I truly believe I would not be able to be the strong, passionate, and positive person I am today. I was extremely shy as a child, and alopecia forced me out of my shell. It was like I always had this strength inside of me that was only exposed once my hair was gone. Losing my hair helped my strength shine through.

I had long, slightly unmanageable hair. It was a perfect blend of the delicate, thin strands I got from my father and the abundant volume I received from my mother. Losing all of that in a couple of months was so new and scary. The summer after the start of my alopecia, and the start of my eighth-grade year, was when my hair started falling out more rapidly. What started as quarter-sized spots had expanded and I barely could cover them with the palm of my hand. The powder I mentioned in a previous chapter was just not cutting it anymore. Many thoughts filled my head. Would my friends see the bald spots? If they did, would they say anything? Would they even stay friends with me? Would I be bullied? These questions consumed my thoughts daily.

As if middle school puberty wasn't enough of a punishment, I also had the added layer of dealing with my hair loss. I tried desperately to maintain the hair I had left, but it was no use. With my parents freaking out, I felt even more lost and alone. It was scary going through all of these emotions by myself and having no concrete clarity of what was going on. At such a young age, when you already question your looks, losing my hair caused me to feel unattractive. I felt like I wasn't pretty enough. Being a typical thirteen-year-old, I was boy crazy, just like most of the other girls in my class. *How was I ever going to get a boyfriend if I didn't have pretty hair? Or any hair for that matter?* At that age, you aren't thinking about adult problems, like taxes, bills, wrinkles, or the potential of hair loss.

I felt so unattractive I did not want to leave my house. No girl should feel that way. This image of a skinny model with luscious hair society promotes was not who I saw every time I looked in the mirror. When I would brush my teeth, I would always keep my head down so I would not have to see my reflection. I've even tried covering up my mirror with a towel, but I would catch a glimpse of myself every time I tried to put it up so I gave up because there was no point in doing so.

I know a lot of people think *it's just hair*, but people who suffer from hair loss lose something that is a much bigger part of their identity. Femininity, sexuality, attractiveness, and personality are symbolically linked to a woman's hair, more so than for a man. Hair loss can therefore seriously affect self-esteem and body image. In a study titled "Psychosocial Consequences of Cancer Chemotherapy for Elderly Patients," which detailed cancer patients with and without alopecia, those with alopecia had a poorer body image (Nerenz et al.,1986). Furthermore, women's self-concept worsened after hair loss. Their self-esteem decreased as they saw their hair fall out. I hit a low point when I was left with 5 percent of the hair on my scalp, with only a few patches of hair left. I felt even more ugly keeping it on my head.

My thinning hair gave me the little push of confidence to shave off what was left. At the same time, it was hard to let those last few patches go. What if my hair never came back again? I talked to my parents; I told them I wanted them off my head because those three to five patches of hair were a constant reminder of those agonizing and restless nights of me crying in my room. They just kept bringing back bad memories I did not want to relive. However, there was no way we were going to a public salon to shave my hair off. I could not bear the stares and I would just turn bright-red if I knew other people were watching. Therefore, my parents called up their friend, a hairstylist, and she helped me shave the rest of my hair off in her basement. She had a whole setup of sinks to wash people's hair, swivel chairs, and supplies. People come to her regularly to get their haircuts, but I was the only client for that timeslot. My parents asked to not have anyone present if possible. The drive to her house from mine was less than five minutes, so I did not really have time to let the fact I was about to shave the rest of my hair sink in.

All I knew was this was happening. We arrived and went inside, and I sat in the swivel chair while my parents and sister stood behind me. The hairstylist was getting her supplies ready, and I was anxious. I had mixed emotions, but I could not bear to see the few remaining strands of hair on my head. She asked if I was okay and ready and I gave her a slight smile and said, "*Yes.*" She picked up the clipper and proceeded to shave my head. Once my dad started to tear up, I started to tear up. But mine were happy tears.

I will never forget watching my dad tear up as he watched the hairdresser shave all my hair off. My dad doesn't really show his emotions and doesn't like to admit when he cries. Like the time he helped me move into college, he said the "dust" was making his eye water when he left. The day I took my identity back created a dust storm that liberated me yet broke my heart when I saw my father tear up like that. He cares so much for me and I'm so grateful to have such an amazing dad. My father usually gives off the persona he is all macho, but seeing him cry showed me the vulnerable side of him, and his vulnerability confirmed to me he has emotions that sometimes cannot be hidden. It was the first time I remember seeing him cry.

When the rest of my hair was shaved off, I felt like I had gained my sense of control back. It honestly felt so liberating for me when I finally got rid of the final lingering patches. When my hair was falling out, I couldn't stop it; it just kept falling out after every shower or with every stroke of my comb. Being able to shave it all off gave me a newfound sense of confidence and control. I was able to finally stop watching my hair continue to fall out. I took my power back.

3

GETTING USED
TO THE LOOK

———

Thankfully, the shape of my head is not wonky. I still had a lot to get used to. As liberating as shaving my head was, I was still not comfortable enough to go out in public without a hat or beanie. It was nerve-wracking; I spent every second scanning the room to see if anyone was staring at me instead of being present and enjoying the moment I was living. It was difficult to not feel confident enough to be in the presence of others.

People would stare. Others would point at me and cover their mouths with their hands, whispering to one another behind my back. They would then proceed to laugh. And no, they were not kids. They were fully grown adults. I found this degrading and extremely frustrating. I was thirteen and being made fun of by people triple my age. I didn't know adults could or would do that, and I felt like such an outcast. I thought that was how I would be treated in the future. It was summertime and I was wearing a beanie because it covered more of my head than a cap or hat would. Even now, when I am out with my friends, I always notice stares from others and when I ask if they saw those people stare at me, my friends would reply, "*No way, you're just overthinking it, Steph.*" However, I'm not overthinking it. I bet my fellow alopecians can agree. We are more conscious of our surroundings and always feel others are staring at us because of our bald or balding heads. Having alopecia made me more aware of my environment, always scanning the room to see if people are looking. I also know many people who have pictures throughout their hair loss process to document their journey, but I did not want any pictures of my head. Now, I wish I had taken those pictures to look back to the beginning of my journey. However, at the time, I was so self-conscious of my look. I could not even look at my reflection in the mirror most times. If I had taken those pictures then, I could now see how much I've grown, but at the time, that was never a thought in my head.

All of my friends, family, and people I knew within my community had always seen me with hair. The first time they saw me in a hat, some would be in shock and others would ask me where my hair went. I would smile and play it off, not knowing how to respond, and would tear up and cry a few minutes later. The first time I went to a youth group event at my church with a hat on, a guy screamed, "*Steph, what happened to your hair?*" I responded by crying because everyone was staring at me and my anxiety just went through the roof.

Another instance was when a young adult at church was curious as to what had happened to my hair. He lifted up my hat to peek at my head without my permission. I tend to stay away from confrontation, so I just stood there, taken aback. I'm sure he meant no harm, but it caught me so off guard. I stood there frozen and quickly pulled my hat back down. At that point in time of my journey, I had not shown my bare head to anyone outside my family. When he did that, my eyes frantically scanned the room and made sure no one else was staring at me. It was the first time someone just lifted my hat without asking me and overall a really uncomfortable experience.

I didn't really dress up too much and wore jeans and T-shirts a majority of the time. I was not allowed to use makeup nor did I know how to apply it. One day at church, the new pastor's wife was introducing herself to me. I had become extremely shy after losing my hair and was always nervous around new people. But I mustered up the courage to introduce myself.

"Isn't Stephanie a girl's name?"

Right then and there, I cried. I hid behind my dad so he could shield others from looking at me trying to manage an awkward smile while tears rolled down my cheeks. I don't blame her for not knowing though. It was utterly heartbreaking to me to know someone, and maybe even more individuals, perceived me as the opposite gender since I had no hair. This was the summer before I started eighth grade, so I was terrified at the thought of a classmate calling me a boy. This was a turning point for me in this chapter of my life. I know we often change ourselves to appease others; however, the changes I decided to make, I did for myself.

Purchasing more feminine clothes and wearing makeup helped me regain a sense of confidence. My original wardrobe consisted of T-shirts and jeans with the exception of one or two dresses my mom wanted me to wear at holiday events or church. So, I bought more skirts and dresses. I also bought more accessories such as necklaces and bracelets to go with my clothes. I went through a wardrobe change since I did not want to be called "sir" when I politely held the door for people behind me or browsed through the ice cream aisle at Walmart. However, even when I dressed up, some individuals would still say, "Thank you, *sir.*" I would turn red immediately and look around to see if anyone else heard. I always looked to my sister to cheer me up. My mom did not allow me to apply makeup immediately because she was worried makeup would damage my skin and cause acne. I did not purchase or learn how to apply makeup until my junior year of high school.

I had a hard time getting used to my new look. The process is different for every individual, and it is never the same for two people. One person in particular, congresswoman Ayanna Pressley, had to get used to her look while being in the public eye. Pressley is an American politician serving as the US representative for Massachusetts's seventh congressional district. She set a precedent for women everywhere, especially within her career. She delivered a speech to the House of Representatives in September 2020, discussing her journey with alopecia and how she has come to learn to face this reality. During her speech, Pressley said:

"Some people may say it's just hair. But for me and many people living with alopecia, hair is intrinsically linked to our identity and our cultural expression."

One hundred percent. I now embrace my bald head, but like social media influencer Chloe Bean said, *"Hair is the most visible characteristic of the body. It is a core trait of femininity for women."* Losing the most visible characteristic of the body is difficult, and that journey takes a person on a rollercoaster of emotions. Like me, there were various times when Chloe would look at herself in the mirror and just shed tears from not liking the image reflected back to her. Every day, she would wake up and the first thing she would see is her silk pillow covered in clumps of hair. Imagine waking up every day to find your hair all over the place, not being able to have any control over it. It's frightening and hard not to feel you are losing a part of yourself.

Many people will say "it's just hair" or "you're so lucky you don't have hair." Or even say I am able to save time by not needing to shave my legs, not needing to schedule wax appointments, or even I save money on hair products. I tend to say those things when I'm joking around friends; however, it is insensitive when others make ignorant comments like the ones above. Such comments downplay our experiences and even set us back in our journey. These individuals did not go through hair loss and do not know what it feels like to be in our shoes. I am fortunate to have people around me who made me feel confident in myself; but for others, they don't have that, and losing their hair is like losing a part of themselves. It's hard. My emotions were constantly fluctuating as I went through my hair-loss journey, but I wouldn't have wanted it any other way. Alopecia did change me physically and mentally, but it made me the person I am today.

I was able to come out stronger, like Chloe. We did not view our autoimmune disease as a setback in life, but instead, we looked at the positives. We looked at the brighter side. Chloe stressed having alopecia allowed her to become this young, confident woman who will always have an open mind:

"Hair may be considered a core trait of femininity for women, but not having hair allowed me to find true beauty. I am bald for a reason and although it gets hard sometimes, I have a story to share and a purpose in this life to fulfill."

She could not have said it better. We all have that strength within us from the moment we are born, but having alopecia has allowed us to find it and realize our true beauty. We all have a story to share and a purpose to fulfill.

To end this chapter, I would like you, as the reader, to do a little assignment. We all have a purpose, so I want you to write down any event or situation that was challenging to you. Why was it challenging? What did you learn from it? How can you use that challenge to make an impact? Take these life lessons, learn from them, and grow into the undeniably amazing person you are destined to be.

4

SCHOOL'S BACK IN SESSION

—

First day of eighth grade: one of the most anxiety-filled days of my life. Stepping onto that school bus, leaving the comfort of my own home, and leaving my parents' reassuring arms for eight hours a day was extremely hard. I had no one to turn to at school, or at least I thought I didn't. As soon as I took a seat on the bus, I received numerous stares from my peers since I wore a beanie and did not take it off even when I went inside the school building. *What a rebel, I know.*

My school had a strict no-hat policy, but my mother informed my principal of my condition, who later sent out a school-wide email informing the staff an eighth grader would be wearing a hat and faculty were not allowed to tell me to take it off. Even though the teachers were aware I would have a hat or covering on, I was really afraid a classmate would point it out and say something like, "Why does Steph get to wear a hat inside?" You know that scene in *The Princess Diaries* where Mia gets a makeover and gets her hair done? Then one girl calls her out and the teacher goes, "Rules are rules. You have to take it off, Mia." Something along those lines, you understand what I'm getting at. The thought of that happening was ingrained in my head at all times.

Thank goodness I was never put in that situation; however, I had my fair share of bullies throughout this journey. It was still petrifying to walk through the halls by myself and endure the constant stares. One class, the teacher was taking attendance and said, "Stephanie." I replied, "Here!" My friend turned around and didn't even recognize me. My classmates then asked me what happened; my face immediately turned bright-red and my eyes bounced from wall to wall, scanning the bewildered faces of my peers. I began to tear up, as I was more emotional at the time. Nevertheless, I was able build up the courage to tell them why I lost my hair.

I explained alopecia to them, making sure to avoid eye contact at all times.

That was the first time I talked about alopecia openly to anyone before. Oddly enough, it did help with the stress— well, after everyone turned around and stopped staring at me. It felt good to get it off my chest.

During the first two weeks or so of school, I did not get called any names—just encountered the many stares. Maybe my paranoia was all in my head and these students looked up to me since I was an eighth grader, top of the food chain in my middle school. Maybe no one wanted to mess with an eighth grader, or they had respect for others. It all goes back to respect. People appreciated me for me, so I was able to live my life and survive eighth grade, which ended up being a year to remember.

This was the year I properly met Ms. Julianne Chandler, the teacher who positively impacted me so much along my journey. As the year progressed, she reached out to me. I did know of Ms. Chandler before my diagnosis. I was in band and she was the choir teacher, so I talked to her a few times. One evening, on the night of my sixth-grade concert, I had an interaction with her. I was actually playing with her hair when suddenly she asked me to stop. At that time, I didn't understand why; later, I found out she had a bald spot under the area I had been playing with. A few weeks into my eighth-grade school year, Ms. Chandler pulled me aside during my band class to let me in on a secret: she, too, had alopecia and wanted to help me with this difficult time.

She explained alopecia to me in a personal way only somebody else going through it could understand. Up to this point, all of my interactions had been with people who never experienced it firsthand. She helped me understand it; she had the answers to all my questions and was able to actually comfort me.

I had the basic knowledge of what alopecia was since I had spent my summer days looking it up on Google, but now I had a live person who helped me understand my unanswered questions. She also introduced me to the National Alopecia Areata Foundation (NAAF). This organization serves the community of people affected by alopecia. Their mission is to support research to find a cure or acceptable treatment for alopecia areata, support those with the condition, and educate/spread awareness to the public about this disease.

In an interview with Ms. Chandler, we discussed the rumors that went around her school when she was in middle school. She was called names such as "baldie locks" and experienced all different kinds of rumors, such as her dad taking double-stick tape to groom their dog and then putting it on her head. *Kids are mean.* Another common rumor was she had cancer and was dying or contagious.

"Kids were not allowed to play with me. Like at recess. I was never invited to birthday parties. Not playing with others, on top of being called names, demolishes a child's self-esteem."

Ms. Chandler was made to feel she was not enough just because she didn't have any hair, that she didn't fit society's definition of "normal." A really funny moment Ms. Chandler shared was when her mom used to put gold, sparkly stickers on her bald spots. "Like if they weren't attention seeking enough, now they had gold, reflecting stars on them. So, I could land an airplane." She reminisced with a smile. She was able to find the funny in a sad time during her childhood, and it really encourages me and others to be positive despite this condition.

Knowing she faced many hardships, she continues to live life positively, which inspired me to forget about the negative thoughts and become a more optimistic person. I still keep in contact with her and we continue to text here and there. The support from my teachers, family, and friends helped me show others alopecia does not affect me negatively; instead, it encourages me to be the person I am today.

I started eighth grade without telling my friends about my alopecia, besides one close one—Jacob. He was the only person I told about losing my hair before starting school again. I've known him since elementary school and I could always tell him what was going on. Up to this point, I could tell him just about anything; nonetheless, I was still nervous as to how he would react when I told him about my condition. I was scared he would not want to be friends anymore. However, just the opposite happened. He wanted to help me start a fundraiser and raise money for alopecia.

With the help from my classmates, like Jacob, and Ms. Chandler, I was able to hold a fundraiser where people could purchase shirts Jacob and I designed. I wanted to fundraise as a way to educate others about alopecia and give back to the alopecia community. I cannot stress enough how lucky I was to have such a strong support system. With them by my side, I became more outgoing, set up more fundraisers, and educated others about my condition.

We set up a shirt fundraiser that had the hashtag #AlopeciaStrong with the NAAF logo on the front and the words "Bald is Beautiful" on the back. I was so happy with the overwhelming support from those around me. I distinctly remember an announcement on the loudspeaker that said, "Whoever purchased shirts for Stephanie, please meet in the courtyard for the picture." Over forty of my classmates and teachers met in the courtyard and we took a picture. In the end, we raised over one thousand dollars to donate to the National Alopecia Areata Foundation.

I had been so hesitant and nervous to even talk about my condition since I was diagnosed with alopecia that same year. My peers are the ones who helped me feel comfortable enough to be open with my condition. Because of them, I was able to overcome this hurdle and come out of my shell rather than hide in it. I was less afraid and able to finally show my true self. My parents and family were, and still continue to be, my rock, but I always felt family members were obligated to say I looked pretty, or I was rocking my look. However, my peers are the ones who made me comfortable enough with myself to let my personality shine through and not worry about my physical appearance. They listened, supported me along the way, and gave me that boost to be myself and teach others.

I continued to hold fundraisers during my high school years through my own club. I started the Alopecia Awareness Club with the help of my teacher, Ms. Mauritzen. She was the first teacher I felt comfortable talking to in high school and I asked her to be the advisor for the club. To my surprise, she had a friend who has alopecia and was glad to be the advisor. Our goal was to spread awareness about alopecia throughout our school and community. Through the Alopecia Awareness Club, we held numerous clothing fundraisers, bracelet fundraisers, household items fundraisers, and dine-to-donates (where the restaurant donates a portion of the money earned that night when a flyer is presented) that allowed us to donate over two thousand dollars to NAAF.

We also held the *infamous* popcorn fundraiser. We started it my freshman year and since then, many people looked forward to that time of year. We had an abundant amount of flavors from sweet popcorn, such as vanilla, caramel, and chocolate, to savory popcorn, like butter, cheese, or salsa and cheese. At only three dollars a bag, we made a killing with this fundraiser. It was by far where we raised the most money. Some teachers and friends would stock up and buy over ten bags. We never ended this fundraiser raising less than five hundred dollars.

From my experience, fundraisers are an impactful way to educate others about alopecia. Every time we held one, people would ask what the fundraiser was for and which club was running it. I could proudly answer, "It's the Alopecia Awareness Club, and our goal is to spread awareness of alopecia to our school and within our community." This always led to them asking more questions about what alopecia was, giving me the opportunity to really educate them about the condition. Fundraisers seem to create this sense of unity. I don't know what it was, but just seeing people come together for a common goal or cause made the whole process extremely worthwhile.

PART THREE

5

STEREOTYPICAL AND
SOCIAL STIGMAS

———

Not all bald women have cancer. That's a stereotype many people immediately picture. Some women are bald because they are emboldened and decide to shave their head, or they could be experiencing side effects of medication or treatment, or they could be like me and have alopecia.

In today's society, we rank the importance of physical appearance and attraction at a fairly high position. Society puts women with long and luscious hair on a pedestal. Society associates a bald woman with having some type of sickness. Like many others going through this disease, I want to negate and debunk this mindset. I am not defined by my disease nor does hair define my beauty. I am not sick; I just don't have hair. When people approach me in public places when I'm out with my friends or family and proceed to ask if I'm okay or how my treatments are going, I stand there in awe of the fact people have the audacity to ask someone those questions.

Not having hair affects an individual's physical and mental health. Alopecia can be associated with serious psychological consequences, particularly in relation to anxiety and depression (Hunt and McHale, 2005). A study conducted by two lecturers in psychology and biopsychology showed women were shocked, embarrassed, and felt a loss of a sense of self when they lost their hair. People with alopecia may feel they are a victim to stigmatization. Yes, alopecia is not life-threatening nor does it inflict pain on one's body, but it does cause a great deal of emotional stress and low self-esteem.

Many people say, "It's just hair." I am truly grateful this condition does not have any effect on my health, but it is not "just hair." Research shows people with alopecia have higher levels of anxiety and depression, and they also experience lower self-esteem, poorer quality of life, and poorer body image (Hunt and McHale, 2005). In relation, their sense of identity is hindered; sexuality, attractiveness, and personality are linked to a woman's hair. Hair is a form of expression. Individuals express themselves through music, art, or by the way they dress. Many people do not realize it, but hair is a *huge* factor when it comes to expressing themselves.

Losing your hair is difficult for anybody. Bald men feel they can't show emotion because it's "normal" for men to go bald as they get older. As it does with women, hair loss "affects the balding individual's feelings of attractiveness and satisfaction with his physical appearance (body image) and can influence other people's perceptions of him" (Stough et al., 2005). Male-pattern baldness has been often referred to as the cancer of the spirit. "The retreating hairline, which is the most common symptom of androgenetic alopecia, or male pattern baldness, often contributes to a man looking older. This seemingly small change can cause a dramatic loss in confidence" (Hall, 2019). As emphasized in "The Psychological Impact of Male Hair Loss," research has shown hair loss can lead to a feeling of unattractiveness and even, in some extreme cases, a body dysmorphic disorder where a person has overwhelming anxiety about their appearance. Most men feel they have to act tough, like nothing is wrong, because they have to be "masculine" and show no feelings. That is very untrue. Men are allowed to cry and be upset when losing their hair. We need to normalize men showing emotions when they are upset.

Moreover, we all need to normalize bald women. Seeing a bald woman in public doesn't mean she's sick or contagious. I have been so lucky to become a part of such a strong community of alopecians through the Naked Confidence Campaign. We have weekly hangouts where we discuss life and its problems and look to each other for advice. Listening to some of the stories, I am baffled at the way my community members were treated in school, in their workplace, or in public. Many times, I heard stories of strangers making fun of someone, calling them names like "cancer head." Yes, you heard that right! Random people were making fun of a bald person for having cancer. And *what if* that person had cancer? Is it even right to make jokes about a person going through *cancer*? Once I heard that, my jaw dropped and I was absolutely shocked. Ms. Chandler had to face these mean comments at such a young age. She was only ten years old when she heard the rumor that spread around her school she had cancer and was dying. Anyone with a heart would know those comments are just ignorant and rude. Who says those type of things? Insensitive comments like that cause my hope in humanity to lessen.

I was fortunate enough to receive some words of wisdom from Dr. Angela Rodgers. She was diagnosed in childhood; however, it wasn't until college she lost most of her hair. She was outgoing, working at the dining commons on campus in her pre-med years, but when she would go home every night, she helplessly watched her beautiful, curly black hair swirl down the drain, then cried herself to sleep.

"None of my housemates, classmates, or family knew I was suffering and broken inside. I was ashamed and felt alone. I didn't know who to turn to or how to get help," she said. "Years later, during medical school, I found a psychiatrist who helped me realize my value had nothing to do with my hair. I learned I had to nourish and strengthen my mind while I got used to my new physical appearance. Then, I had to learn how to love myself again."

Loving myself again. That hit home. I didn't feel pretty when I had hair and felt even more unattractive without. My family always said I looked beautiful, but I felt like they were obligated to say that. My friends probably didn't think I was ugly; nonetheless, I never received the verbal affirmations, such as "You're so pretty," compared to the other girls in my grade. That's one of the reasons why I think I look for reassurance when it comes to something as simple as choosing outfits or something as important as completing job applications. I haven't found that maximum level of confidence within myself to make me trust my own decisions and believe in them. My self-esteem did decrease a significant amount during my first year with alopecia, but through the people I have met and the decisions I made for myself, I regained a sense of confidence and began loving myself. Now I don't have to cover my mirror with a towel to avoid my reflection, and even though I have some off days, I react with a huge smile upon seeing myself.

Everyone's journey with alopecia is different, but we typically go through the process of "finding" ourselves again. We lose something that is such a big part of our identity and it's hard to rebuild our confidence and self-worth. We all go through our journey at our own pace and will love ourselves again, even if we need a little push from others.

Dr. Rodgers has shared many insightful gold nuggets with me. She also mentioned, "Not many people consider the psychosocial impact of alopecia, which is the emotional, psychiatric, and mental health aspect of the disease; instead, the first typical thing that comes to mind are the types of medication they might need." We need to break these patterns.

For the past ten years, Dr. Rodgers has been the alopecia support group leader for Sacramento, California, and has just begun cohosting a webinar series for women with alopecia titled *Let's Talk*. She takes so much pride in her work because, best of all, she is a family medicine physician who "has the honor to teach patients every day they are not their disease." That last line really resonated with me. Teaching patients they are not their disease is what allows them to make the best out of life and not let their disease hinder them. That is exactly what my dermatologist, Dr. Castelo-Soccio, did for me.

She helped me prevent alopecia from defining who I was and what I was capable of doing. The message we are bigger than our disease is so impactful and sticks with us throughout our journeys. Dr. Castelo-Soccio knew of many medications and treatments that could treat alopecia. Some have had amazing results where kids would get a full head of hair. However, the treatments always came with unknowns because they were in the trial phase. I was scared, but I was also at a point in my life where I recognized alopecia only affected my hair and nothing else. I did not want to go through treatments and put my life at risk for the possibility of cancer in the future.

Having Ms. Chandler's insight and the respect of my community, I did not feel the need to have my hair back. At the time, did I want my hair back? Most definitely. I wanted to fit in. I wanted to do my hair like the other girls. It was difficult, but I am fortunate I was surrounded by people who did not make me feel hair was my most important characteristic. Every time Dr. Castelo-Soccio brought up recent treatments that were in the trial phase, my parents were eager for me to try it. But I surprisingly stood my ground and said no, I am *happy* with the way I am. Dr. Castelo-Soccio never encouraged or pushed these treatments onto me and even praised me for loving the way I am.

Society has created the stereotype bald women are sick and unattractive when compared to women with luscious, long hair. However, more women are taking control of this stereotype in hopes of putting an end to it. The message of body positivity continues to spread, with some women shaving their heads for personal reasons, with no underlying medical reasoning. Whether it is culture, religion, environment, or a medical condition, the number of bald women is increasing. "Shaving my head" is now a bucket list item for many. Numerous individuals across all social media platforms take videos of themselves, documenting the experience of shaving their heads and hoping to inspire others in the process.

Despite all this positive energy around bald women, many alopecians receive backhanded compliments like, "You are pretty for a bald girl."

I had the opportunity to speak with social media influencer Nicolas Roman Srut, whose TikTok videos offer a funny perspective about alopecia and make people laugh while spreading awareness about our condition. We discussed the aforementioned comments he receives via social media or in person. People don't realize it is somewhat degrading when we hear these comments. They think it's a compliment, but it really isn't. "You are pretty for a bald girl" or "You are handsome for a bald guy" is another way of saying you're pretty even though you have a disease. He also emphasized the fact it is not even exclusive to alopecia, for people will get the same ridiculous and ignorant backhanded comments for other conditions, such as vitiligo or albinism. Sometimes it's even a matter of race, such as "You're pretty for an Asian" or "You sound so sophisticated for a Black person." It's like people are afraid to admit they like something that's different or something that is not normally accepted or regarded as beautiful. It's unacceptable, yet we have engraved in our minds and allowed society's definition of "normal" to affect our daily lives.

One haunting example sticks out to me. It's a viral video of a twelve-year-old girl, where she is pranking her mother by putting on a bald cap. The mother's reaction to her "shaving her head" was also outrageous and staged, pretending to faint. These behaviors are unacceptable and degrading to the individuals who actually have to go through this. "These actions harm our progress to self-love," says Kylie Bamberger, an alopecia advocate who became viral due to her bridal pictures where she's embracing her baldness at her wedding.

Kylie's goal is to spread awareness about the condition and along the way help people be true to and love themselves despite what society says.

The bald cap prank video upset many members of the alopecia community and we did not let it go. Numerous individuals commented, reposted, and reported the video, letting the influencer know it was not a joke. This video was humiliating for so many bald women like myself. Pretending to be bald should never be a joke. Millions of individuals are bald, whether it be from alopecia or chemotherapy. Someone may be bald because of cancer treatments, and mocking someone because they're sick is disgusting.

We struggle with finding confidence and courage to go out in public bald, and this video just validates the reason why so many people are scared to embrace their true beauty. This individual has over two million followers and through that video, she sent the message being bald is some type of joke. It's not.

As Christie Valdiserri, first ever *Sports Illustrated* model, always says, "*We need to normalize bald women!*" An increase of bald pranks is surfacing on the Internet via YouTube or other social media platforms, and it's not funny. Imagine the little kiddos who follow these influencers and watch these type of prank videos. How do you think they feel when they watch it? Terrible. And it's not just kids, but adults, too, who are going through this rollercoaster of emotions. We're asking why we're different and why our condition or the way we look is being made fun of.

On the brighter side, society is now becoming more accepting of women of all shapes and sizes, but every generation still needs to try harder. We need to teach each other to care and love everyone, regardless of gender, race, or socioeconomic status. With all the hate that is going on in this world, we have a responsibility to be the light and pave the way for future generations to follow. Everyone is on a different journey, filled with ups and downs, and we need to respect each other because we never know when we'll encounter a person pushing through one of their downs.

I always aim to remind myself *I am not defined by my hair,* but it's hard when society puts one body type on a pedestal, and you feel like you won't be able to fit the image. At times, I get emotional seeing women style their hair, just them using a comb, curling iron, or straightener, knowing I might not ever be able to do that if my hair never grows back. Wigs are just not the same. The mindset I try to live by is to *be**you**tiful.* I am still me and you are still you and no one can change that, but we can embrace it.

6

BULLIES — DON'T HATE, ALOPECIATE

———

It was the second week of eighth grade. Like I have previously mentioned, I was exempt from the no-hat rule at school, so I walked in that morning as I had for the past two weeks, wearing a beanie. With it being the start of the school year, I'm sure you can relate, it's usually pretty warm outside. This day was exceptionally toasty. As you can imagine, I was hot and extremely uncomfortable with sweat accumulating under my beanie and dripping. I brought a paper towel along with me so I could quickly wipe under my beanie when no was watching. I'd take being hot and uncomfortable over showing everyone my bald head any day. I wore a beanie for the entire school year. I still wasn't brave enough to be bald in public. It's nerve-wracking. I felt naked when I took off my beanie or cap, even at home around my family. So, facing people outside of my house was even more terrifying.

People must've thought I was stupid, that I couldn't possibly hear them two feet from me. Putting their hands over their mouths, then proceeding to whisper to someone else, not even hiding the fact they were gossiping.

When I walked to class, I usually had a friend to walk with. Having a friend by my side allowed me to feel safer. I hated walking by myself; I always felt like everyone's eyes were following me. Yet with a friend, I could put those worries aside and have a companion to talk to, distracting me from the stares. However, there were always some classes where I was by myself and had to bravely face the dreaded hallways. I always looked down; I didn't want to make eye contact with anyone, and when I did look up, people were scanning me. It makes me uncomfortable now just thinking about it. I had a simple and effective game plan: eyes down, walk briskly.

This method worked great in middle school, so I thought this strategy would be effective to survive ninth grade, but there was a possibility my method would no longer work. High school is another level of stress; more people means having a potential for less forgiveness, and I needed a more solid backup plan. I was in the highest grade in my middle school and maybe that is why I was shown respect. I would be the freshman, a.k.a. fresh meat, as soon as I walked through the daunting high school doors.

When I entered high school, I still wore a hat but would change up the styles. You would think people mature as they get older. That's not always the case for some individuals. I don't know if their parents just didn't raise them to have manners or be kind to others, or if they just wanted to act tough. I thought high school would be better than middle school, but my freshman year started out shitty. A few months in, I was waiting for my friend by her locker at the end of the day so we could catch the bus together. As I stood there on my phone, a senior walked past me and flipped my hat off my head. I know, *what a dick*. I went home crying that day. I started tearing up on the bus, unsure of where to look. My friend sitting across from me on the bus asked if I was okay, but I could not get any words out. Instead, I texted her what had happened. It was a six- to eight-minute bus ride from school to my house. There were a few stops before my street; it typically didn't take long. But that day, the bus ride felt like an eternity.

Once the bus pulled up to my stop, I quickly ran off the bus, making sure not to make any eye contact. I sped-walked home as fast as I could and closed the door as soon as I went in. I could not hold back the tears anymore and let them all out. My parents were coincidentally working from home that day and ran to me once they heard me crying. "What happened?" my mom scream-asked. Trying to get the words out between breaths was not easy. After calming down a bit, I told them the whole story and my mom threatened to sue the school. I told her not to call because I did not want to draw any more attention than I already was. My mom, being the overprotective and crazy yet loving mother she is, did it anyway. She called the principal and reported the incident. The next day, I was called down to the assistant principal's office and told this was not an act of bullying. Being the timid freshman I was, I replied with a head nod paired it with an *okay*.

I wish I had been able to stand up and advocate for myself at the time. However, I am a strong believer things happen for a reason. Although this was not an easy situation to be in, I became a stronger person because of it.

Later in my freshman year, I was approached by Mr. Levi, a physical education teacher who also coached basketball and soccer for our school. One day, during class, he stopped me and asked me to try out for the freshman basketball team. Mr. Levi always had a positive attitude and a smile on his face that brightened my day. If he had never encouraged me to go try out for the basketball team, I would not have met some of my closest friends.

To this day, I am still not sure why Mr. Levi asked me. I love sports, but I had never touched a basketball before tryouts. Maybe it was fate. It was tryouts for the girls' freshman team, so it was basically walk-on; however, I wouldn't have tried out if Mr. Levi hadn't approached me that day. To my surprise, I didn't suck too bad. I made some baskets and was able to understand and execute the drills, except for left hand layups. They get me every time. Running up and down the courts was also no bueno. Cardio and I are not the "bestest" of friends. A few days later, the coaches posted the roster of the girls who made the team and guess who did? *This gal!*

During scrimmages and games, I was not allowed to wear a hat. The coaches and athletic supervisor went to the state board and went through a process to attain a paper that permitted me to wear a bandana instead. So, shout out to Mr. Ryden, Coach Nash, and Coach Hagensen. They didn't have to do that for me. They could've easily said I would have to play without any head coverings, but they went through that process, and it meant so much to me. I was truly grateful to have such great friends and faculty because I could have had a totally different high school experience.

I sometimes sit and think of all the things that wouldn't have happened if certain events hadn't occurred. For example, our school district had specialized high schools we could test into. Students could attend one of two vocational schools— Biotechnology High School and High Technology High

School, where you could specialize in the sciences. Other schools in our district had different interests people could test into. For example, one school would be the designated culinary program, one would be geared toward science and engineering, and another would be ROTC, and so on. I took the placement test to get into biotechnology; however, I did not get accepted. Notice how I didn't say "unfortunately." It's quite the opposite. If I had gotten accepted, I most likely would have enrolled in that school. But I didn't get in and due to that event, I met many people I am proud to call my friends. If I had gotten in, I would not have met the amazing teachers and staff I came across during my years in high school. I would not have been involved in the various clubs I had the opportunity to be a part of. I could not imagine life without the genuine individuals I met in high school. Being rejected from the specialized school was the best thing that happened to me. It blows my mind, but I wouldn't change it for the world.

As previously mentioned, things happen for a reason. If I had not accepted my bald self and worn wigs, I might not have been made fun of. If I had not been teased, I wouldn't have been forced to accept who I am through my humor. Had I not accepted myself and allowed myself to feel happy, confident, and supported, I'd never have become an advocate for others with alopecia. I am a strong believer things happen for a reason. That bullying instance happened to make me stronger. Me being diagnosed with alopecia gave me a way to shine a positive light on others with the same condition.

7

BROW GAME: WEAK TO FLEEK

———

My brow game should win most improved. I didn't apply any makeup whatsoever from the time I lost the hair on my eyelashes, eyebrows, and basically my entire body in seventh grade until my sophomore year of high school. I didn't know how to draw eyebrows or apply any other types of makeup. It wasn't really a priority for me at the time, so I didn't invest my time in watching and learning from YouTube videos. Now, I can't even attend virtual classes on Zoom without makeup on. Wearing makeup definitely gives me a sense of confidence—like the lipstick effect phenomenon, as discussed in "Can Wearing Makeup Boost Cognition as Well as Confidence?" a known psychological phenomenon in which wearing makeup can give individuals a confidence boost by making them feel more physically attractive, and increase feelings of self-esteem, attitude, and personality. I feel better about myself when I have makeup on.

My mom wasn't much help in the makeup department either. The extent of her makeup routine was applying eyeshadow. She did not know how to apply eyeliner nor draw on eyebrows. Me being an artistic person, I kind of just winged it at first, drawing on eyebrows and putting on eyeliner. In lieu of YouTube videos, I looked at pictures on social media and based my eyeliner off what I saw. Starting off, I used an eyebrow pencil to draw in my eyebrows, which looked *alright*, but they weren't good enough to look on fleek. I then discovered this waterproof powder, which I applied with a brush to draw on eyebrows which helped tremendously. I could now jump in a pool without having to worry if my eyebrows were going to drip or disappear.

Sometimes, despite my best efforts, I simply could not get my eyebrows right. They wouldn't match, or one would be higher than the other, too thick, or too thin. It used to make me so frustrated; angry tears would roll down my face. I would not want to leave the house until they were up to my standards.

One morning, before heading to church, I just could not get them right. I got to a point where I cried and threw a fit and delayed my whole family from getting there on time. Of course, my family was annoyed and frustrated I was not ready; however, it also made them sad they could not help me draw them on as well. I really wanted to get my eyebrows done. I was tired of not getting my eyebrows right every morning. My parents never understood the full extent of my frustration. I begged them to let me get them done, but it was not until my pediatrician recommended to me to get my eyebrows microbladed my parents agreed to at least get a consultation.

Microblading is a tattoo technique that involves a small blade with ten to twelve little needles at the end that applies semipermanent pigment to the skin. The artist mimics natural eyebrow hair strokes, leaving flawless symmetrical eyebrows. With the phone number for a lady named Lang, who my pediatrician had recommended, my mom and I anxiously called to schedule an appointment. I was seventeen at the time, and Lang was hesitant at first since she had never conducted microblading on anyone as young as me. At last, she agreed and I could not contain my excitement.

I was super nervous to get them done, but it would save me so much time in the mornings! I wouldn't have to get up an hour earlier in case I was not able to draw on my eyebrows in twenty minutes. I was constantly in a time crunch every morning before school. I would set my alarm for 7:00 a.m., yet snooze it and tell myself five more minutes. Well, the five minutes would turn into fifteen minutes and I knew I had to get up when I saw 7:15 a.m. illuminate on my phone. The bus arrived at my stop around 7:55 a.m., give or take. So, I only had forty minutes to brush my teeth, put my makeup on, get dressed, and eat breakfast. As I would do my makeup, I'd hear my mother yell, "Hurry up," and the added stress would not help me draw on my eyebrows the way I wanted them. Microblading would definitely ease the stress of trying to get ready on time for school and not miss the bus.

My parents, especially my mom, would ask me why I wanted to get my eyebrows microbladed and what was the difference between that and a wig? My mother would say, "They're both cosmetic, right?" Yes, they are, but they are not the same thing to me. One of them made me feel like I was hiding myself under it while the other would help me boost my self-esteem. To this day, she doesn't truly understand my reasoning. I think she has learned to accept my look and knows I love the way I am. *I wanted* to have eyebrows and having them would definitely allow me to be more confident in myself.

With my appointment date approaching, my anxiety was soaring through the roof. Finally, it was microblading day. I laid anxiously as she applied the dye to my skin to test if I was allergic to it. After seeing I did not have an allergic reaction to the dye, we proceeded to the microblading procedure. She drew on the measurements and numbed my eyebrows. Once I was all numb, she continued with the actual microblading. It was such a unique feeling; I couldn't feel anything, but I could hear the little lines being created. As she continued with each little stroke, I kept reminding myself I was one step closer to having the perfect eyebrows I'd always wanted.

When it was done and she revealed my eyebrows to me, it was the first time in a long time that when I looked at my reflection in the mirror, I knew I was beautiful. When I went home that day, I went through so many emotions. I cried tears of joy and I was so relieved I did not have to carry the weight of worry, the weight of spending an unnecessary amount of time trying to perfect my eyebrows. I could now go out in public with my eyebrows on fleek every day.

8

HIGH SCHOOL: DREADING IT TO MISSING IT

————

The first day of high school felt like I was starting all over again from scratch. My last year of middle school felt safe, but now, I was in a brand-new jungle. Walking in, I was nervous, had sweaty palms, and was unsure of where to go and who to talk to. I was still wearing a hat, but my sense of self-esteem diminished. I didn't have my close friends there as my support system. Some of the kids in this high school were nearly a foot taller than me, which made me feel so small, in every way, just vulnerable.

My best friend and I were acquaintances throughout middle school, but we became closer during high school. On the first day of ninth grade, I tapped Gisella on the shoulder as we were walking through the lobby; she turned around and smiled, but she did not realize it was me. She thought I had cancer, like many other people. It wasn't until later that year when we had a world history class and physical education together she talked to me about a homework assignment. From there, we became classroom buddies, sharing class tips and information, and our friendship grew. I was able to talk to her about my life with alopecia so far; she was supportive, listened, and helped. We bonded over our mutual love for sushi and sports, and now, I have one of the greatest friends anyone could ask for.

My classmates didn't know how to approach me either, but a few brave souls asked why I was bald, which gave me the opportunity to explain my situation. I hoped more people would ask me about my condition instead of assuming I had cancer.

Even now that I've been out of high school for some years, people still assume I have cancer. I'll be in the supermarket or the mall and they will walk right up to me and ask, "Do you have cancer?" I like to educate others on my condition and would prefer a, "May I ask you what happened to your hair?" I guess that's better than the people who just say, "Oh," and walk away. In all honesty, I prefer the ones who compliment me and say things like "I am gorgeous" or "beautiful." That always makes my day.

High school now seems like such a blur. The time flew by so fast. I know it's cliché, but cherish the time in high school. Before I knew it, I was accepting my diploma on the football field and heading off to college. It was filled with numerous ups and downs. Yet luckily for me, I had more ups than downs. I was section leader of my school's marching band, manager of the girls' varsity and junior varsity basketball teams, vice president of National Honor Society, president of Spanish Honor Society, president/founder of the Alopecia Awareness Club, and a member of Anytown (a selected group of students who taught others about the issues of bullying and drug use through skits and informational sessions), and to top it off, I was in my school's pit band.

I was able to participate and get involved in the extracurriculars my school had to offer because the other students at my school accepted me for who I was and did not judge me based on my physical appearance. You're probably asking yourself, "Why does that have anything to do with me being involved," right? Well, you see, without their respect, I would have let alopecia hinder me from participating in things like any other "normal" kid and longed to go home as soon as the last bell of the day rang.

That's one of the reasons why I was able to thrive and be myself throughout high school. I did not have to be subjected to name-calling and I appreciated that more than anyone could ever know. I was bullied once, but others who have alopecia probably end up being diagnosed with depression since they do not have that support system or their daily life at school just sucks because of kids who are ignorant and are not mature enough to understand hurting others to feel better is not how you do things. Most of the research shows people with alopecia have higher levels of anxiety and depression than those without. They also experience lower self-esteem, poorer quality of life, and poorer body image. Those who lose eyebrows and eyelashes may also have problems with identity and identity change, as these features help to define a person's face (Hunt and McHale, 2005). I don't know why bullies decide to bully people. In my opinion, they find joy in ruining people's days just so they could have the satisfaction of feeling "superior."

As discussed in a previous chapter, I was never given the name of the guy who flipped my hat off my freshman year, so my friends went on a mission. I saw the back of the guy who flipped my hat. He was tall and had dirty-blond hair. My friends took that information, put their Instagram investigation skills to work, and found him. For privacy purposes, I cannot tell you his name. I've always wanted to know why he never apologized. Even though I was put in this shitty situation, I came to realize I have some pretty badass friends.

I was also so blessed to have teachers I could trust and talk to. I could always turn to them when I was upset or feeling down. When I had arguments with my mother about wigs, I was upset and unsure of how to feel. My teachers always lent their ear and heard me out. Some being mothers themselves, they helped point out how my mother might have perceived the situation. They had my back and always made sure I was okay.

I participated in my school's marching band and we wore our uniforms and a hat with a large plume at every game. When we would change into our uniforms before each game, I would quickly change from my snapback baseball cap into the marching band hat. This was my ninth-grade year, and after weeks of practicing, we headed onto the field for our first game. Up until this point, I had worn a hat to school and practice every day since my alopecia started. I was excited to play; however, I had not thought about the entire process of a game...the national anthem. As soon as the announcer said, "Please take off your hats as the marching band plays the national anthem," time froze, and I could see myself from the outside, wide-eyed and sweaty, just waiting to see if the other band members also took off their hats or if this was just something the crowd did. Everyone else in band took off their hats, and I was having a full-on internal meltdown. I didn't want anything to do with alopecia in that moment. I was not sure what I should do, but in the spur of the moment,

I ultimately wanted to be respectful, so I decided to take it off as well. For the duration of the national anthem, I was frantically looking around me to see if anyone else was looking at me and my bald head. To my surprise, nobody even looked at me, at least I didn't think anyone saw me.

Me and my head—I used to separate the two. I used to distance myself from my alopecia because I didn't want people to see me and just label me as the "bald girl" before getting to know me. I never showed anyone, aside from my family, my bald head until my junior year of high school. I decided to stop wearing hats; as aforementioned, I was part of my school's marching band and the semi-circle tan lines on the back of my head were not the most flattering thing. The first few days of not having my hat on was extremely terrifying, but it got better from there. My friends complimented me on the perfect shape of my head and it made me feel more comfortable with myself.

One of the most surprising influential moments of my life happened a few months into my junior year. I was walking through the hallways from one class to the next and suddenly, someone ran past me, rubbed my head, and screamed, "I need luck on my math test!" I was very taken aback by it, but it made me laugh.

I had many firsts in high school; for the first time in front of my high-school friends, I wore a wig to my senior winter concert. I don't know why, but I feel like I received more stares when I was wearing it versus when I was bald. At the same time as the concert, my friends had basketball practice and some didn't recognize me and walked past me, including my best friend, Gisella. I think it was when my friend, Nocco, realized it was me underneath the wig and said with her jaw dropped, "*Steph*?" Everyone else stopped in their tracks, turned around, and were equally surprised. They were hyping me up and saying I looked so beautiful and it put such a big smile on my face. In that instance, I was happy to be complimented, but I will always think, *Was I not beautiful without my wig?*

However, the biggest smile I ever received in high school was from an elementary classroom. The summer before senior year, I volunteered in a 21st Century Community Learning Center program in a neighboring town where I taught computer skills and Chinese Yo-Yo to at-risk elementary and middle school students. These kids were so energetic and they put a smile on my face every time we had class. I continued to teach Chinese yo-yo in their extracurricular program after school on Tuesdays. I looked forward to seeing them every week. Later into my senior year of high school, the superintendent of the school district approached me and invited me to read to a first-grade class where one of the students, Dante, also had alopecia.

It was such an amazing experience and seeing Dante's smile was just so precious. On Twitter, his teacher posted an activity the class participated in the next day. It was a fill-in-the-blank worksheet that said "I like _____" multiple times. Dante filled out the blank with "myself." It honestly brought me to tears when I read it. At such a young age, I'm glad he was able to say, *I like myself.* Even now, I have trouble here and there with saying I like myself with so much confidence. A lot of individuals said he must have been really happy to see me, but in reality, his courage gave me more confidence to go about life with a positive attitude, and it made me so happy to see I could make a difference in his life, even if it was the slightest bit.

Seeing him happy made me realize my potential to help others. I went from wanting to have nothing to do with alopecia to loving myself. Dante gave me the courage to keep pushing on and helped me carry myself with a positive attitude.

9

NO HAIR = BEST HAIR

———

Who would've thought I would go on to win Best Hair for my high school's senior superlatives? For those of you who don't know what senior superlatives are, they are "awards" or "titles" given to two seniors for each category that embodies the serious and funny aspects of the class. My school's superlatives ranged from "Best Sense of Humor" to "Most Likely to Succeed."

What made me want to run? I thought it would be funny for a bald girl to win best hair. I did it as a joke but didn't think I would actually win it.

A week went by and then the voting period was open. I opened the Google form and saw my name under the category "Best Hair - Female." I was taken aback and thought, *Dang, I got a shot at winning this.*

I then posted the announcement on my Instagram story to tell people to vote for me and to my surprise, it blew up. People swiped up, hyping me up, and others came up to me in school the next day saying I got their vote. I accomplished the unthinkable. The first ever bald girl in Marlboro High School history to win best hair.

I was so happy when I heard the news! Ryan, the male winner, and I excitedly started brainstorming our ideas for the superlatives picture day. These photos would be shared in the yearbook. We landed on creating a fun sign that read "We woke up like this" and during the photoshoot, we had the photographer take various pictures of us "twirling" our hair, even though I just looked like I was making the "she's going crazy" gesture. The contrast was perfect—Ryan with his long, Fabio-like hair shining in the light and me with my bald, beautiful, shiny head. We had a blast. Everyone around had such a good laugh watching us pose; it was such a memorable experience. It definitely makes the Top Five highlights of my high school career.

Speaking of Best Hair, a memory that has always stuck with me was when I was seventeen years old. I was at the mall, checking out of a store, when the cashier complimented me saying, "I love your hair." My initial reaction was that of happiness; who doesn't like a good-hair-day compliment? But *what hair*? Nonetheless, I knew what she was referring to, so I paused for a split second to process what she had just said and I, in turn, smiled and said, "Thank you." She loved my hair, so I guess it does really come to show no hair = best hair.

TO WIG OR NOT TO WIG?

That's the real question. Wigs come in various styles, colors, and lengths. They are a way women can express themselves. When it comes to hair loss, wigs may help people gain a sense of confidence back. Hair loss diminishes self-esteem, and it may be hard for people to go out in public. In order to cover up their bald or balding heads, both women and men alike can find synthetic or human hair wigs that are styled the way their hair was once. Or they could change it up with a new style and color! People might want to wear wigs to bring back that sense of comfort and familiarity.

However, I wanted to go to senior prom without a wig. I wanted to go to prom as myself. Plus, wigs were very itchy and uncomfortable for me. Leading up to prom, I had such a long argument with my mom about wearing a wig. She wanted me to wear a wig to prom and I clearly did not. During our argument, her reasoning for a wig was so I could change up my look and "dress up." This argument carried on for two weeks. At one point in the heat of the week, I became so emotional about the situation I started crying during lunch. Looking back at that situation now, I understand my mother's point of view. Many mothers and motherly figures hate to watch from the sidelines as their child loses their hair, helpless and unable to do anything about it.

Luckily, I had people I could rely on and talk and vent to about my problems. One of these people, Ms. Tsakiris, my marine biology and zoology teacher, was always there to listen and I felt comfortable talking to her. She had words of wisdom and helped me see the other side of the situation. Most importantly, my sister, Tiffany, is my rock. I can go to her whenever I have a problem and am able to rant to her. Even though she is younger than me, she does give some pretty good advice. If I didn't have the people I could talk to and I had to keep my feelings to myself, I'm sure I would've cried and broke down even more.

The buildup of anxiety from the week before prom to the day of prom was astronomical. I had never worn the wig I wore to prom before. No one had ever seen me in it and I was beyond nervous. I had only worn my other one before—a short-hair-styled wig. I didn't know how others would respond to this one. It was a long, dark-brown-haired wig.

The day of prom. None of the girls wore makeup that day so we could all have a fresh face for the extravagant prom makeup once we were out of school. I think that was the only day I ever went out in public without makeup since I first started applying it. My microblading was a tad faded, so I filled in my eyebrows, but other than that, no other makeup products were on my face whatsoever. The entire day, I walked around avoiding eye contact with people; I was so afraid of my peers seeing me without makeup. All the seniors were let out early in order to get ready for prom and get dressed for the big event.

After school was a rush. My parents drove me to the mall for my makeup appointment. The stylist did a gradient light-green to darker-green to match my emerald dress and she applied fake eyelashes. Since I had never worn fake lashes before, the feeling was definitely strange at first. My eyelids felt so heavy, but looking in the mirror, I was in love. They looked so good! My daily makeup routine does not consist of putting on a full face of makeup, yet for prom, I went all out. This meant my face foundation did not match my head. The stylist was about to start applying it on my entire head before I stopped her and mentioned I was wearing a wig for the evening. Once I was done with makeup, we rushed home. I had a pre-prom party at my house, which is a small gathering for prommers to take pictures and get some food in our bellies before the main event. I quickly got dressed and with the help of my little sister, we styled my wig.

After the parents snapped all of the necessary photos, we headed off to prom at iPlay America, an arcade and amusement center. Well, prom was held in the warehouse of iPlay, but it was still fun and memorable nonetheless. As I walked in and saw my peers, a good handful did not recognize me with the wig on. Some just walked right past me and didn't notice who I was. Some of them stared and were like, "Steph, is that you?" There was also one instance where one of the teachers who sat with me at the scorer's table for basketball games, Ms. Caruso, knew who my prom date was and when she saw him enter with me, she didn't realize it was me in the wig until she looked at me more closely. I found it so funny and will remember that moment forever.

I received tons of compliments at prom and they really bolstered my self-confidence. Every time someone complimented me, it brought a smile to my face. Yet I always wondered if I would have received the same compliments if I did not have a wig on. I guess we'll never know. Don't get me wrong though; receiving those compliments made me beyond happy that night, but it does make me wonder sometimes.

On a side note, I'm not sure if other alopecians or bald people ever experience this, but when I wear a beanie or a hat, people have a hard time recognizing me. In college, when it was cold outside, I would wear a beanie to keep my head warm, yet when I said hi to people, they would wave back but have no clue who I was.

It was so nice to receive multiple compliments on my wig at prom, but I felt like I was hiding under there. I know many people who are able to pull off different looks each day of the week, yet I did and still do not like the way the wig rubs on my head, even if I have a wig cap underneath. Since prom, I have not worn my wig, even for special occasions. I love my bald head and as an added bonus, I can catch the breeze when people with hair can't.

No Hair = Best Hair. Having alopecia comes with its own benefits. Not only are we saving the planet by taking shorter showers, but we also get to save money on hair products.

All joking aside, Deeann Callis Graham said something us alopecians can 100 percent agree with. Alopecia gives us the "ability to develop strong relationships not based solely on our appearance." Wife, mother, published author of *Head-On, Stories of Alopecia*, small-business owner, public speaker, and life coach, Deeann has gained a following since she started her podcast titled *Alopecia Life* in 2018. She has over fifty episodes that feature guest speakers who offer advice or share their inspirational stories. Both her book and podcast have positively impacted so many individuals. Alopecia has allowed us to build quality relationships with quality people.

PART FOUR

10

FrUsTrAtEd BUT THANKFUL

———

Out by my locker as an eighth grader, I was grabbing a few books and noticed a girl three lockers down. She was mindlessly brushing her hair before her next class. I went to reach for my own hair that should have been laying in front of my shoulder, but nothing was there. The first thought that came into my head was, I can't do that anymore and I may never have another chance to brush my hair. Sometimes the simplest tasks would make me emotional. I would see girls in my class aimlessly twirling their hair while they worked on their class materials or listened to the teacher. I'd catch myself getting upset over it. These little things definitely made it hard for me. School dances were especially difficult. My friends, with excitement in their faces, would proudly show me the hair styles they loved, and I'd smile and compliment them; however, inside, I was upset.

After days like these, I would go home and head straight to my room. Knowing my parents would be frustrated if they saw me cry, my room provided a safe place to cry in silence.

No one in my family understood what I was going through. I would have episodes where I was genuinely sad and go to my room and cry. I now realize part of their frustration was toward themselves not knowing how to help me feel better. However, at the time, I thought they were frustrated at *me* because it was one of those times where I was "in my feels" and wanted to cry. Since I felt this way, it was difficult for me to express my emotions around them freely. Most of the time, I would cry in a secluded space so they wouldn't see me. I wanted to avoid them asking me. Like I mentioned before, I would not be able to express myself in front of them. It may have come off as being closed off to my parents; I felt responsible for their emotions. I did not want to ruin their day just because I wanted to cry. So that's the reason why I would cry alone—to avoid the whole situation altogether.

These self-doubting issues made me reclusive and I felt like I could not share it with my family; they just wouldn't relate to it. I became exasperated with the people around me since no one else knew how I felt. I didn't know how to make myself feel better about my image and I struggled with discovering my self-worth. I'd become annoyed with people around me, taking my frustration out on them. I didn't yell at my parents, but I would talk to them in a condescending tone, or even in a negative manner. I understand they just wanted to help and simply didn't know how to. All the emotions would just build up and I would want to cry again. So, if Kleenex saw a rise in sales from June 2014 to October 2014, it was because of me.

I clearly remember the first time my parents took me to buy wigs. It was the summer of 2015, before eighth grade. My hair was falling out rapidly at this point, and I did not know how to deal with my look. At this time, all I wanted was my hair back, so I agreed to go wig shopping. I do not recall the name of the shop, but the woman who ran it was very patient with my family and me and showed us a variety of wigs. She would happily go to the back and grab more until I found one I was okay with. I didn't know if they looked good, and of course, my parents said all of them did. I felt they were obligated to say all of them looked amazing, so I didn't trust their opinion. As I tried on the wigs, I felt like it wasn't me and I was hiding. To add to the uncomfortableness, they were extremely itchy. I also love playing football and basketball with my family and friends, and it would be so tiring when I was simultaneously sweating and making sure my wig stayed on my head.

I want to quickly pause and say I am beyond grateful for all my parents have done for me—from buying wigs to driving to doctor and acupuncture appointments. I really cannot thank them enough. I know they care about me deeply; however, I felt like I was left out of the decision-making process sometimes. I didn't want to wear wigs. I didn't want to go see doctors and acupuncturists. Yes, I wanted to know what alopecia was and the facts behind it, but I was not and am still not a person who seeks treatment for it. I constantly felt my parents and family were 100 percent for treatment and I wasn't asked how I felt about them.

I did not recognize their efforts until I was a little older. I do appreciate it even more now. At that time, though, between hospital visits and discussions about wigs, I focused primarily on the negative side of things. They did everything possible in order to allow me to feel "normal" around others. I know they were just trying to do what they thought was best for me. So, if you are a parent of a child who has alopecia, my advice is this: ask them how they feel and what they want to do. I know some parents want to do everything in their power to help their child grow hair because that's what they think will make them feel "normal" or okay again, but that might not be the case. Ask them and support them in how they want to go about their alopecia journey. Communication is so important and it will help your child shed light on how they are feeling and open your eyes to new perspectives you may not have considered.

Fortunately for me, a few months later, I met Ms. Chandler, whom I shared about earlier in the book. I really mean it when I say she changed my life when she pulled me aside during class. If she had never reached out, I would not have known someone else who could relate to what I was going through. I have another fond memory of Ms. Chandler I'd love to share. She was aware of how I was struggling to express my opinions with my parents, so one fall evening, she came over to my house with her own mother. Her mother shared her struggles with having a child she could not protect from alopecia. She talked to my parents about the bullies Ms. Chandler had to face and her journey with alopecia, as well as the resources and support groups they turned to during this unprecedented situation in their lives. Both of these women went out of their way to help my parents and me improve our relationship and life for the better. Even now, I can turn to Ms. Chandler when I'm in need of advice or if I want to talk to her about my bad day. I hope you as the reader can also find strength in another alopecia partner and you can both help and guide each other through difficult times.

11

MASKS ON

———

We all have masks on, whether it's putting on a smile even though you're having bad day or using makeup to cover up acne or blemishes on your skin. For many alopecians, we turn to wigs to mask ourselves. For others, a wig is a form of expression and they rock the look flawlessly. Some people can switch from blonde one day to brunette the next, or have longer hair one day and execute a shorter look the next. However, for me, I viewed wigs as a way to hide my "imperfection" or "insecurity." Makeup, on the other hand—I couldn't and still can't go out in public without my eyebrows or eyeliner drawn on. Makeup is definitely my crutch.

Talking with Kylie Bamberger, social media influencer and alopecia advocate, helped me realize it's a matter of how someone chooses to use their mask. People may wear masks to hide their feelings or pretend to be something they are not. However, it shouldn't always be viewed in a negative light. A person's "mask" may be something he/she/they use to conceal some aspect of themselves to make them feel better about themselves. She mentions "wigs are a really good mask"; however, she always wore it to make those around her comfortable.

I also had the opportunity to speak with Kevin Bull, professional "obstacle athlete," independent stock trader, and businessman. You might recognize him from the television shows *American Ninja Warrior, Spartan Team Challenge*, and *Team Ninja Warrior.* He mentioned support groups acted as a crutch for him. He felt they hindered his progress to becoming confident in himself. To him, support groups "are really how you accept something; it's something that at times for me became a crutch. You know, I would feel bad and then I would go and experience the sympathy from my support group. I think the giving of that sympathy actually caused me to take a little longer than I would have to accept [alopecia] without it."

I never thought about it that way. For me, support groups and having someone to talk to who related to what I was going through helped me. Although support groups did make Kevin feel better at the time, he found "there's an interesting balance and eventually you have to be able to say to yourself sometimes you're not ready. You know? It's to go down that path of accepting something you don't like, and having that support group does make you feel better and maybe saves you some mental anguish of being forced into it too quickly, but eventually you have to make the decision yourself, the decision you're going to accept it. And that part of the journey is very individual."

Very true. At the end of the day, I had to muster up the courage and confidence to accept myself and be my true self. To this day, I still have some off days. When I see my little sister braid her hair and go shopping with my mom for hair products or when I see girls do their hair, it does get me in some kind of sad mood. These days, it's easier to brush off these sad feelings and relish in the memories of everything

I have overcome and the sense of value I have achieved. I am able to show my true self to others, and not many people can confidently say that.

In 2020, at the age of nineteen, I was part of the Book Creators Program where we had the wonderful opportunity to attend speaker sessions and listen to a vast range of individuals—from actresses to best-selling authors to comedians and more—who told their story. One speaker in particular, Tiffany Haddish, said something that really resonated with me. "*Stop trying to fit in with people who don't even know your last name.*" Let that sink in.

As a kid, I always wanted to fit in with the "popular" kids. In elementary school, during recess, I wanted to play kickball with the "cool" kids. It didn't help at this time of my life, I was also a very chubby child, therefore, I was picked last every time. So that was definitely not helping my confidence. Then, when I lost my hair, I wanted to "fit in" more than ever. I just wanted to be viewed as "normal." As an eighth grader in middle school, I was so preoccupied with worrying about what others would think of me because I didn't have hair. I was so preoccupied with worrying I did not have time to reflect on myself and build myself up. I was a very timid and shy middle school kid.

That all changed after my alopecia, believe it or not. Well, not instantaneously, as you have read. But, with the help of Ms. Chandler's guidance, I was able to find confidence in myself and embrace some aspects of my alopecia. Then, with the kindness and respect of some of my peers, I was fortunate to build friendships with people who saw past my appearance. If Tiffany Haddish had been there to tell me to stop trying to fit in with people who don't even know my last name, my journey might have been a little smoother. In the end, as Kevin pointed out, a journey is very individual and it is our decision to make—to learn to accept the hardship at hand or let it have power over us.

Another inspiring individual I had the opportunity to interview is Anthony Carrigan. The actor and TV personality who plays NoHo Hank in HBO series *Barry* and Victor Zsasz in *Gotham*, grew up having alopecia. Alopecia made him insecure and he would try to hide it. He had hair until his mid-twenties, but all of a sudden, it fell out. When he went to auditions, people noticed he was balding. He started getting fewer callbacks and meetings. The industry stopped wanting to hire him. So, he had a decision to make—either give up or change the business. With a lot of willpower, Anthony was able to pave a path for others and set a precedent that appearance does not take away from his skills and personality as an actor and a person.

Anthony was able to change the business, but it wasn't smooth sailing from the get-go. He experienced many ups and downs, just like anyone going through a hardship. He described his crutch as the attempt to blend back into a society that ostracized him for his appearance. He drew on eyebrows to try to conform to the standard of "normal" society has placed on us. During his early stages of alopecia, he would go into auditions and his lack of confidence would show. Many times, he was rejected and told "there was just something wrong with his face" and he wouldn't fit the role.

"I think the issue can be you trying to change yourself to fit societal norms because you're terrified of the alternative. When you're doing so because you're so worried your alopecia is going to somehow make you not enough and ostracize you from your community, from society. Ultimately, my crutch was trying to

blend back in. Blend back into a kind of business that ulti-mately wasn't really having it anymore."

Once Carrigan made the decision to truly embrace his look and make it his own unique trademark, things started to change.

"That's when people were like, oh, wait, actually, that's really cool. So, it was kind of my acceptance of alopecia that let them accept it as well in a sense, you know?" During my interview with Anthony, the thing he said that stood out most to me was, "It's going to take little baby steps toward self-acceptance and embracing alopecia...[but] just so you know, it's gonna end up being your golden ticket. It's gonna end up being the thing you love most about yourself."

So true. I used to question why I had to lose my hair. I was already this Asian girl who didn't know what fashion was and I was on the heavier side of the spectrum. I've been bullied for my weight and now this. Losing my hair was extremely difficult, but Anthony could not have said it better. After accepting alopecia and loving myself, I was able to show off my personality to others and finally be myself. Alopecia is what I love most about myself, and embracing it allowed me to see life in a different light.

When I lost my hair in middle school, all I wanted was to be seen as normal. We all go through things to feel normal again. But what is normal exactly? According to ReviseSociology, normal can be defined as any behavior or condition which is usual, expected, typical, or conforms to a preexisting standard (Thompson, 2018). Every person is so unique and we cannot fit one single definition of normal or be bound by what others deem as right or ideal. Therefore, being ourselves and embracing who we are is what's most important.

In addition, you have to play to your strengths. Since I'm bald, there's a plethora of bald characters or people I could dress up as for Halloween. It all started in my senior year of high school. We had this parade called the Spooktacular Parade where the marching bands and dance teams of the various schools in the district would participate. We all chose our own costumes and dressed up for that day. I went as Caillou, a popular children's TV show character, and received so many compliments. People from other schools also came up to me and said they loved my costume. That day, I knew I'd found my calling.

During my freshman year of college, we had the perfect "Halloweekend," a three-day weekend—Thursday, Friday, and Saturday—where college students dress up for Halloween all three days. I was only able to participate two days out of the three, but I dressed up as Aang from *Avatar: The Last Airbender* and Mr. Clean.

For the first night, Thursday, I went out as Aang and my friend, Victoria, helped paint the arrow on my head and arms. When we were done getting ready, we headed outside to take a bus to College Avenue, a campus at Rutgers. As I was walking down the streets of New Brunswick, I felt like a movie star; people who I did not know at all asked to take pictures with me or of me. I was uncomfortable at first, but I got used to it, "hair flick." The costumes I picked helped me embrace my alopecia and those iconic bald characters.

The Friday of Halloweekend, one of my friends, Susane, whom I met earlier that week, snapchatted me and asked what I was going to dress up as that night. I replied with "Mr. Clean" and she was super hyped for the costume. When I finished painting my eyebrows white, we headed to the bus stop once again. She was there and screamed, "*Mr. Clean!*" It took me aback, but I literally felt like I was bombarded with paparazzi. It was all fun and games, yet those few nights meant so much to me. I really loved having people appreciate my costumes, yet what I loved the most was others seeing my personality and confidence through my costumes instead of the bald aspect of me first.

Due to the COVID-19 pandemic being in full force in 2020, I was not able to execute the costumes I had planned for Halloween my sophomore year since the whole world was in quarantine. I was so excited to dress up for Halloweekend again as Pitbull, a member of the Blue Man Group, and Charlie Brown. Those costumes are waiting in the closet until the day I can bring them to life.

Other amazing costumes I had the pleasure of seeing from fellow alopecians are Voldemort from *Harry Potter*, Gru from *Despicable Me,* and Dr. Evil from the *Austin Powers* film series. We used our baldness to our advantage and pulled off such awesome costumes, and most importantly, our energy and personality shines through each and every one. I was able to let my personality become something people knew me by instead of my appearance. When I learned to embrace my look and love myself, I was able to radiate positivity and feel so much better about myself. It was difficult, and there is a rollercoaster of emotions that comes with the process, but being able to be true to yourself is the best way to carry yourself every day.

12

CONQUERING MY FEAR...OF DATING

———

You have a match! Those are the words many women and men receive when they are use online dating or dating apps. They're also the words that terrify me. To this day, I'm still nervous to try online dating in fear of rejection because of my bald head. So many women and men are scared to date due to the social stigmas and norms we face daily. So, I would like to pose these questions: *Do men and women find bald women attractive? Do men and women find bald men handsome?*

In a conversation with social media influencer Nico Srut, he mentioned he feels like he gets fewer matches "than you know, maybe a guy who's good-looking or is as good-looking as I am who has hair, maybe even not as good-looking as I am, but he has hair. He gets more matches. And it's like, although that might be true, it does mean I get more quality matches." He notices guys who are less attractive than him receive more matches than him due to the fact they have hair. However, here comes the bright side of it—right off the bat, he gets matches with decent people who see past the baldness and are more focused on someone's personality.

As I was looking for answers to my question, I came across this website titled Love, Alopecia which features one story about being a bald woman in the dating world. The author of this post stated one thing that stood out to me: "Women are more disturbed and mortified than men at the thought of a woman having no hair. Funny that! It's ironic society has us believe no matter what we do, we just aren't good enough. We have been taught to fear and hate ourselves, to be in competition with others and ourselves constantly. It has been ingrained in our belief system from birth; every sense of our self is under judgment" (Love, Alopecia, 2020). So maybe I've been in a competition with myself constantly and scared to venture out of my shell?

I guess I'm scared of rejection. I know there are plenty of bald men and women who are in relationships or are married. However, when I was in eighth grade, I knew a boy who liked me and I liked him too, yet he told my friend even though he really liked me, he didn't want to be seen with a bald girl. That was the only reason. The fact somebody would be too embarrassed to be seen with me because I was bald hurt and it has stuck with me since then. This traumatizing event, at an already impressionable age, has been part of the reason why I'm so scared to put myself out there. I'm so scared of not being liked solely based on my appearance. We could be vibing and have our interests align, but the only reason it wouldn't work out is because of how I look. And I know what you're thinking: they're just not worth my time. I would say the same thing to someone going through the same emotions as me; however, the truth is it hurts and plays with your mind. I've always pondered this situation:

Say I was wearing a wig in public and a guy approached me. We just felt like we had a strong bond and as our relationship progressed, I would reveal my bald head to him. But my looks didn't matter to him because he accepted me for me. However, if I didn't wear a wig in that given situation, would that same guy still approach me?

It just makes me wonder. I know online dating is becoming more popular nowadays. I'm also afraid people will just judge on appearance since they don't know my personality before deciding to swipe right or left. However, after talking to Nico, I decided he did make a good point—that quality matches come in because they see past appearance and want to get to know you for you.

So, I did it. I put my fears aside, and with the support from my friends, I created an online dating profile on a popular dating app my sophomore year of college. It was absolutely nerve-wracking for me. Uploading pictures and inputting my answers for various prompts was a scary process. I was on FaceTime with my Gisella as I was going through this entire process, and there was a point where I just wanted to call it quits and delete the app, but just as I was about to give up, my sister came into my room and pressed next on my screen for me.

What are sisters for? My little sister, Tiffany, pushes me to be out of my comfort zone at times. She has always been the only one I feel comfortable talking to about my insecurities or problems. I could just turn to her if I felt like crying. Although she didn't know what I was going through, she would sit there and listen. I felt sometimes my parents weren't the easiest to talk to because they wouldn't know how to respond and, in that moment, I felt like I was a burden and taking up their time. But Tiff would let me vent out all my problems and hug me when I needed it most. Having someone listen to whatever you're dealing with is the best medicine. Just talking about anything and having that person or group hear you out and genuinely care about what you have to say works wonders. I am so grateful for my sister and would have no idea where I would be now if I didn't have her by my side.

With Tiff's support, I finished and posted my profile, and I received several likes within twenty-four hours. I guess Nico was right about the quality matches. They clearly saw I was bald; nonetheless, my amazing personality shined through my pictures and my quality answers painted a realistic persona of what I was like as a person, which these matches appreciated. Seeing those likes definitely boosted my confidence. Those guys found me attractive even though I did not have hair, but it is my friends and family I owe to helping me find that confidence. They helped me put myself out there and their support means the world.

My perspective of myself has changed after using some dating profiles. I went from thinking I'm unattractive to I am *beautiful*.

13

JOKE'S ON YOU!

———

Humor. It's something we all use in our daily lives. Some use it to make others laugh. Some use it to heal themselves as a coping mechanism. I joke about my baldness and condition because it helps me cope with it. I'll make comments such as "I don't have to shave" or "couldn't be me" when someone talks about their hair routine or haircuts. I honestly can't remember the number of jokes or little statements here and there about my head, but not everyone is a big fan of them. Some people might not know me as well and feel uncomfortable when I make a joke; however, the people who aren't the hugest fans of the jokes are my parents.

They do not appreciate the jokes at all. When they get haircuts and I say, "I have not had a haircut in six years!" they quickly respond with "You will," coupled with a look. You know, *the* look. The eyes staring into your soul like you said or did something wrong. When they react that way, it makes me feel like they want my hair to grow back and are hopeful it will. During the first few years of my diagnosis, they frantically searched the Internet for remedies or various doctors, acupuncturists, and specialists in hopes of finding someone to help "cure" my alopecia. Sometimes I feel like they don't fully accept my alopecia. I've had this condition for almost seven years, yet they long for the day my hair grows back again.

When my sister would buy numerous, and I mean *numerous*, hair products, I would make a lighthearted statement I'm saving my parents money since I do not have to purchase all these hair care products. That statement is typically followed by the statement, "Don't say that!" I proceed to question why they would say that and they say I will need it in the future. What if I don't? I'm perfectly okay not having to spend money on hair care products and I love the way I am.

"Am I not pretty without my hair?"

"You are, but you would be even prettier with it."

Immediately, my smile turns upside down. It's quite difficult to find confidence when you have family members tell you you are prettier with hair. I fight that internal battle every day, questioning if I am pretty enough for the guys my age or if I would be prettier with hair. Personality is what matters, but it hurts to hear things like, "You would be prettier with hair," especially when it's coming from your parents. This is not to bash my parents; they probably aren't thinking how it could affect me before speaking. I, too, am guilty of not thinking before acting. My hope is sharing this conversation may offer insight to parents, relatives, or friends of alopecians, that my fellow alopecians do not have to hear these words from anyone.

But what if it doesn't? Or what if it does grow back, just to fall out again? I've accepted it and am proud and happy with who I am. Of course, I have those days when I'll get sad after looking in the mirror and not feeling like I'm pretty enough, or having my parents react so quickly to my jokes, and the "you will" doesn't help my confidence either. I like me for me and feel like they haven't accepted the fact it might never grow back, so it's degrading at times. I feel like I'm at a constant battle with myself, just not knowing how to think or feel. A part of me wants to be confident, which pulls me in one direction, but the quick reactions from my parents pull me the other way. So now, I'll just avoid making jokes in front of my family altogether, or else I'll just get the look again.

However, I'll still make little jokes or comments around others. I love making others laugh, and making bald jokes about myself does just that. One study discussed how women and men felt about their alopecia and how humor was used during their process. "Females experienced greater feelings of loss, were more concerned about their looks and their future, and reported more negative thoughts and emotions. Females felt angry and blamed God for their fate; males blamed both their fate and luck" (Rafique and Hunt, 2015). Coping with humor was typical of males in this study; they made fun of themselves in front of friends before their friends could joke about them.

Theorists suggest "laughter and humor are instinctive coping mechanisms that help people deal with the disappointments and struggles of life. Specifically, it is believed by finding humor in stressful or potentially threatening situations, people can replace negative with positive affect, thereby giving them an increased ability to cope with negative states of affairs. Humor based on incongruities, or things that appear inappropriate for their context, is particularly well suited to reappraising negative situations from different, less threatening perspectives" (Wilkins and Eisenbraun, 2009). Another point made by researchers was "humor may be beneficial when and if an individual has accepted their condition and is feeling very positive about their situation" (Rafique and Hunt, 2015).

I can definitely relate to that. I started making jokes my senior year of high school when I felt comfortable around my peers, but first and foremost was able to make jokes when I was confident in myself. However, I do have to admit when non-alopecians make those joking comments, I feel uncomfortable; they never went through what I experienced and it creates this awkward vibe and atmosphere. By inputting their own assumptions of bald people into the mix, it comes off more offensive than it does funny. People assume bald people do not know how to braid hair because they don't have any, or all bald people go through the same experiences. They assume bald people wish they had hair and are unhappy. They assume bald people have weak immune systems, so therefore, we have cancer or are sick, even contagious. Some of the alopecians I have gotten the opportunity to talk to said while they were working as servers in a restaurant or bar, their customers would request a different server because they thought their server was contagious. Sometimes alopecians get free food and benefits when going out since people assume they have cancer. That's never happened to me before, but hey, for those who have been in situations like that, why not make the best of it?

Alopecians typically encounter at least one person who comes up to them and asks if they have cancer. I guarantee it. It has happened to me quite a few times; nonetheless, it's nice to be able to educate others about my condition. However, in one instance, a woman approached me and asked if I had cancer. I replied with "No, I have alopecia." She replied with a disappointed, "Oh," and walked away. I was about to tell her all about alopecia, but she was *disappointed* I didn't have cancer and walked away. "I'm sorry, what?" I just stood there and was so confused at what had just happened. I replayed the situation in my head and asked myself if I had said something wrong; I guess the lady did not get the answer she was looking for.

Anyway, onto my favorite assumption—that we can't be or aren't feminine. I recall seeing a post on Instagram where a woman was holding a sign that said something along the lines of *Alopecia took my hair, but not my femininity. Yes.* Just because a woman lost her hair, it most definitely does not make her less feminine. This goes for bald men too. Not the feminine aspect of it, but that balding and bald men are not old and are not aging quicker than others. They might just have alopecia. Bald men and women are still themselves. They are still amazing individuals. Hair does not define who we are as people. We are still us. People who think we are less than the person we were before our hair loss are oblivious to the power of personality and energy. People with that mindset are not worth our time if they cannot see our true selves before coming to conclusions based on appearance alone.

Aside from making jokes, I also play to my strengths. In my senior year of high school, for college commitment day, my sister covered my head with glitter. I committed to Rutgers University and cut out a template of the letters "RU." She taped the "RU" on my head, applied hairspray to the back of my head, and then had at it with the glitter. The glitter look was a hit and caught everyone's eye when I walked throughout the hallways. I was happy to see people staring at me. I held my head up high to flaunt my sparkly head. If I told my thirteen-year-old self I would be walking around with a head covered in glitter, I would have never believed me.

Another fun memory of that year was when I put eyes on the back of my head. I had some googly eyes left over from a project in marine class. These googly eyes were not the peel-off-the-tape kind. Somehow, the oil secreted from my scalp allowed the googly eyes to stick to the back of my head so I could have "eyes on the back of my head." It was very entertaining for me and those around me.

Using humor and my baldness as a positive helped me gain confidence and block out the negative people in my life. Smiling and laughing is contagious. When I see someone smile or laugh, it automatically puts a smile on my face or I start laughing along with the person. I always try to have a positive energy because it affects those around me and hopefully makes their day a little brighter.

PART FIVE

14

I'M A CAP KID

———

I would like to preface with this: I am not a great public speaker. I tense up and become so nervous I am unable to form coherent thoughts. When I try to talk, a bunch of jumbled words come out of my mouth.

I was invited to speak at Alopeciapalooza, a three-day camp where alopecians of all ages come together to share their experiences and do fun activities with one another. At Alopeciapalooza, it may be someone's first time meeting another person like them and with all of those heightened emotions, it's overwhelming. I was fortunate to have known seven other people in my town who had the same condition as me. Some people may be the only Alopecian within a one-hundred-mile radius of their town and never meet someone like them.

Alopeciapalooza 2021 was held in Quarryville, Pennsylvania. I was so nervous and excited for this event. My parents drove two hours to Quarryville, but I made them leave before I spoke. I wanted them to be there; however, I knew they would just criticize me after speaking. I know myself, and I know I would have been more preoccupied with what my parents would say about my speech and not focus on my actual speech full-heartedly. Once they dropped me off and headed back home, I felt a huge weight lift off my shoulders. It was very nerve-wracking to meet so many new people, yet somehow, I felt comfortable and *not* out of place. This was my first Alopeciapalooza, so I did not know anyone there. It was all so new but so familiar at the same time. It was such a crazy mix of feelings.

I've never been in a room with ten alopecians, let alone over one hunred people with the same condition. With COVID-19 restrictions a bit more lenient, we did not have masks on, so I could not hide my awkward smile. I had my notecards all written out and ready to go. I probably rehearsed my speech twenty times. Jeff Woytovich, founder of Children's Alopecia Project (CAP), introduced me and called me to come up to the podium. Walking to the podium, I was so anxious my legs almost gave way.

I introduced myself and started with a joke: "I have alopecia universalis, which means I do not have hair anywhere, except for one leg hair. My friends and I named him Gerald." With the audience laughing, that calmed my nerves down. I usually stutter and stumble on my words when I have to give presentations at school or speak at various events within my community; however, this time was different. I didn't stumble on my words. I was able to actually make eye contact with others and talk to them instead of burying my head in my notecards.

During Alopeciapalooza, kids and adults can hang out with one another at various planned activities. Some activities for Alopeciapalooza 2021 included archery, arts and crafts, glow-in-the-dark dodgeball, basketball, talent show, and campfire night!

The talent show was the highlight of my experience at Alopeciapalooza. Seeing all these children embrace their alopecia made me feel so warm inside. One act in particular, Sophia, a nine-year-old girl, danced to *The Greatest Showman's* "This Is Me." She came in wearing a fedora as the song began to play, but at the words "this is me," she took off her hat and threw it to the side and had the biggest, brightest smile on her face. Immediately, my friends and I lost it. Danica, Annika, Annie, and I were crying and physically shaking in our seats. We were sitting in the second row, so all the parents behind us saw us. I couldn't turn around and have them all see my tears running down my face; I am an ugly crier. After the performance, though, as I looked around, there was not a dry eye in the room.

Five people were invited to speak during Alopeciapalooza 2021. They usually have more, but COVID-19 restrictions limited the number of speakers. Every story was so insightful and inspiring! One speaker who resonated with me was twenty-three-year-old Annie Leiding. She has spoken at Alopeciapalooza since 2018. She lost her hair when she was a sophomore in college, and it was rough. She had lost all of her confidence from hiding her alopecia from everyone. She was bald, wearing a wig or a hat, and it affected her mentally, physically, and emotionally. Annie is now a mentor and alopecia advocate. She inspires both children and adults alike. When I heard of her experience with alopecia, it really moved me because I could relate. It's hard to explain our feelings to those around us since they would not understand the things we've gone through. Although no journey is the same, we had something in common and we were able to recognize the struggle and more importantly, connect with each other.

These kids are so brave at such a young age. They are such an inspiration, and I cry just thinking about how courageous they are. Like Annie said in her speech, *"Everything happens for a reason."* If I never had alopecia, I would not have been at Alopeciapalooza nor would I have met the amazing individuals I can proudly call my second family.

15

THE NEW GENERATION OF ALOPECIANS

———

Becoming an *influencer*. This coveted title has motivated numerous individuals to pursue careers through the use of social media. Many want to be part of influencer culture. What is that, you may ask? An influencer is an individual who has the power to affect the decisions of others due to their authority or knowledge in a certain topic with their audience by actively engaging with them. In an interview with BBC Three, Dr. Danielle Wagstaff, a psychology professor at Federation University Australia, said, "Social media and influencer culture can sometimes lead us to derive a false sense of what everyone else is doing and this can definitely have a negative effect on our mental health and wellbeing" (Day, 2019). Essentially, she argues we tend to compare ourselves to others on social media, which can make us feel like we're not good enough. This, in turn, can have a massive impact on our self-esteem and increase anxiety. The problem with influencer culture, she says, is we're being fed a false view of what is normal, in terms of appearance and success, and our regular old lives just can't compete.

Social media has such a huge impact on people around the world. In 2020, over 3.6 billion people were using social media worldwide. Instagram, TikTok, Snapchat, Facebook, Twitter, and YouTube are just a few of the social media apps people are using today. On each of these platforms are influencers and celebrities who have huge followings. Their followings consist of individuals who range from young children to older adults.

"One important way this affects us mere social media mortals is body image" (Day, 2019). Everything we see on social media is not always real, yet most of time, we can't help but compare our lives to the influencers' lives. As Dr. Wagstaff mentioned, we are fed these false views of what is normal in terms of appearance and success and we think we just haven't met those standards, yet long for it. Comparing ourselves to others is so harmful to our own self-esteem and progress to confidence and self-worth.

This was brought up a few chapters ago, but influencers who film themselves pretending to be bald and someone's negative reaction to the "new look" are hoping to gain likes and be funny. They might not mean harm and are not trying to send a negative message, yet it ends up being just that—harmful. Even after having people reach out to them and express how the video has affected them, they don't always listen and *still* keep the video up and respond harshly. It is beyond unacceptable.

When individuals proceed to keep the video and ignore the impacted individuals voicing their concerns, their actions are extremely degrading and wrong. As discussed earlier, a young influencer created this bald prank video that involved recording her mom fainting after seeing her daughter's bald head. Her parents allowed her to upload that video and were insensitive to a whole population of bald girls and women. They were insensitive to the fact some girls who have alopecia watch her videos and look up to her. Seeing her make fun of the look they have every day negatively affects their self-esteem.

An increasing number of bald pranks are surfacing on social media and YouTube. One famous YouTuber and influencer, for instance, recently filmed himself being bald for a day. Many thought he actually went bald and shaved his hair off. However, he was wearing a bald cap. There were many mixed reactions from the bald community in response to his video. He did spread awareness about alopecia and felt empowered when he was bald for a day; however, he also included his friends' reactions to his bald head. Many reacted in a negative, shocking way.

Though it was not his intention, it hurts when we see bald pranks throughout social media. Maybe it's for clout, which means having strong influence or power, or the creator thinks it's funny. The thing I would like to point out is they can take off their bald cap at the end of the day. Being bald is a reality for many women and men all over the world. We can't just take off our bald caps at the end of the day. For us, it's not "experience a day in the life of a bald person," it's our reality. It's most definitely not funny when our reality is being made a joke.

On the other hand, Dr. Danielle Wagstaff also stresses "influencers can be a real force for good." Influencers have the ability to spread positive messages. Through social media, we have seen numerous influencers promote body positivity, speaking out against racism, and fighting for what they believe is right. Dr. Wagstaff added, "When we see other people, just regular people, not necessarily celebrities or traditionally famous people, are living relatable lives—posting about their own body image and mental health struggles—it can help create a sense of camaraderie, a feeling 'I'm not alone, other people understand what I'm going through.'" "Regular" people, who are working nine-to-five jobs or in school studying, can relate to the aforementioned type of influencers. Social media has such power—individuals can help promote or spread important messages with their platform or just connect with others.

Numerous individuals are spreading awareness about alopecia throughout various social media platforms, such as Instagram, TikTok, YouTube, and so many more. Emmy Combs and Alex Youmazzo have gained over six million followers each across their social media platforms. Through their videos and content, they have spread awareness about alopecia. Charlie Alexander Villanueva, former professional basketball player who last played for the Dallas Mavericks of the NBA and is now an entrepreneur based in Texas, has also inspired little kids everywhere. When little kids with alopecia saw Charlie play, they gained a sense of confidence seeing him embrace his baldness on and off the court. It compels them to take off their hat, wig, or beanie and say, "*This is me.*" The same goes for kids when they see Joshua Dobbs, quarterback for the Pittsburgh Steelers, aerospace engineer, and intern at NASA (the National Aeronautics and Space Administration), embrace his look on a daily basis. Another inspiring individual I had the amazing pleasure of connecting with over Instagram is YouTuber and social media influencer Shalice Ader.

Shalice remembered moments when she was in middle school and crying in the bathroom, wishing she had long, pretty black hair like everyone else. Insecurity and struggle with finding confidence and positivity overwhelmed her middle school years. However, "the beginning of junior year was the year I built the confidence and gained strength to start going to school bald...It was a huge weight off my shoulders, and I was happy." One thing she said really stood out to me: she was *happy.* Embracing her look made her happy and she was able to live life. I felt the exact same way when I stopped wearing my hats in high school. I felt free again and it was one of the scariest things I've done, but it was worth it. Shalice has had multiple opportunities to share her words of advice with those who struggle with confidence and continues to inspire others. She constantly reminds herself and tells others to *just be yourself.* That is the most important thing—being undeniably beautiful you.

Seeing representation across social media, in sports, or on the big screen is really amazing for children and adults alike because it gives that reassurance it will be okay and you can achieve big dreams even if you don't have hair. These individuals did not let their hair hinder them from achieving their goals, so why should we?

There is a sense of unity in that feeling of "they get it too" or "they understand what I'm going through." The influencers who send and spread positive and relatable messages show why we're *stronger together.* They bring individuals together under one common goal or topic and strive for greatness as a unified unit—one big family.

16

CHANGING THE FRAME

———

We have to *change the frame*. What does that mean? *We* have the ability to dismantle and negate what society has said. Society has put this notion into everyone's minds beauty does not correlate with baldness. But, it's *our* job to change the world for the better and that's only possible if we do it *together* because there's strength in numbers.

That's one of the reasons why I'm writing this book—*to change the frame*. I want to educate others about alopecia and spread awareness about this condition so people can hear others' stories and gain insight on them. As a bald woman, I felt, and still feel, like I'm not pretty enough. I still feel I'm less pretty than all the other girls in my friend group. I feel, deep down, a majority of girls want to be called "sexy" or "hot." I can't speak for all women, but when we hear those words, they somewhat boost our self-esteem and the way we view ourselves, and I felt I was never viewed that way since I am bald. Bald women are increasingly representing us all across social media, in fashion shows, and in the news. They are beautiful, badass women who are themselves and show bald is indeed beautiful.

In an interview with social media influencer and alopecia advocate Nicolas Roman Srut, he emphasized, "Whatever it is, whatever, 'disability' society told you you had, your disease is actually your greatest strength. Now, what matters is you change the frame."

We are medically diagnosed with alopecia; however, that should not hinder the way we live our lives; it's up to us to decide our path, and either we take the positive road or the negative one. Even after our interview, I kept pondering the phrase *change the frame*. It's in our hands to decide how we go about our lives. It is going to be hard for anyone going through a difficult time, but possibly with help and surrounding yourself with supportive people, *you* are able to turn your path around.

My life could've been miserable. Like, absolutely miserable. When I lost my hair, I cried almost every single night for about a month or so. It was not until I started school, even though I was scared out of my mind, I found people who stuck by me and I didn't have to experience bullying and hate so early in life. I could have shut everyone out of my life and put up these walls around me to avoid any conversation whatsoever, yet I changed the frame and was able to live my best life. I wouldn't change anything for the world.

Speaking of support systems, they are so important, especially during any difficult time. In an interview with Kylie Bamberger, an alopecia advocate and mentor, she told me she ate her lunch in her car pretty much every single day of her junior year of high school because she didn't have that support system. Kylie also shared, "I went through a really heavy round of depression during that time. It was not until my senior year when I really tried to regain a little bit of senior life in high school. I did have a couple friends, but none of them made me feel confident or stuck up for me until I had confidence."

When she did display her confidence, *then* her friends would be able to carry on conversations about her condition; nevertheless, they were never a support system she could rely on. Her friends did not help her feel confident and did not stick up for her until *she* had the confidence in herself. That's extremely difficult for a seventeen-/eighteen-year-old. Having to isolate yourself during lunchtime and not having friends who stuck up for you at a moment's notice can do so much harm to one's self-esteem.

Confidence is hard to find within yourself and it's even harder to build because of the pressures around us—societal pressures, family pressures, and personal mindsets. Kylie felt stuck in her image, trapped between societal norms and her values. She started to notice bald spots when she was twelve years old. She wore wigs until she was twenty-two. In the interview, she stated, "I ultimately realized I was wearing it for other people and their comfort. I never really wore the wig for me." Imagine going through ten years of your life doing something for someone else's comfort. Therefore, Kylie stressed the importance for us to become advocates for ourselves and others, whether it be alopecia or not. I know it is easier said than done, yet that weight will be lifted off your shoulders. Allowing yourself to be your true self is the most beautiful and badass thing you can do.

Changing the frame. Another individual who did just that is none other than congresswoman Ayanna Pressley. In September 2020, she delivered a speech to the House of Representatives and said, "No doubt about it, a bald woman entering a room, entering the floor of the House of Representatives, makes people uncomfortable...Visually, it changes every antiquated, cultural norm about what is professional, what is pretty, what is feminine." Let's just pause a moment to let that sink in.

She *challenged* the cultural norm and did it with a new-found confidence. She never lost sight of who she truly was and with this condition came an experience and opportunity for her to use her voice and show others alopecia did not hinder her from accomplishing great things.

Author of *Head-On, Stories of Alopecia* and host of *Alopecia Life* podcast, Deeann felt it's her calling to help connect people with what they are looking for. She wanted to "help others realize they were not alone—sharing stories was one of the best ways to reach people." This leads us to other reasons why I wanted to write this book. Through my personal experience and the stories from various inspiring individuals, I hope my book can impact others who are going through their own alopecia journeys. Deeann left me with, "Everybody has a story to tell. Some will resonate with mine, and others won't. As we share our stories, we never know whose life we will shift, encourage, or change. Stories have the possibility to change lives."

Hearing and researching other alopecians' journeys, a majority wished they had or did have support groups. It doesn't even have to be a group; just having *one* person to talk to about any troubles or hardships you are experiencing is beyond helpful. Talking with others allows you to vent your feelings and improve your mental health. Having people with the same condition as you or people who are going through what you are works wonders. In terms of alopecia, it is truly amazing to have people on the same level as you and understand what you're going through. It promotes a sense of unity and mutual understanding.

In a study funded by the University of Minnesota, researchers found there is indeed a psychological effect of alopecia areata (AA), but group interaction may help lessen the burden on both the individuals with this condition and their families. This study, titled "Importance of Group Therapeutic Support for Family Members of Children with Alopecia Areata: A Cross-Sectional Survey Study," also found "children with AA may also have a deficiency of peer connections because younger elementary school–aged children were more likely to be uncomfortable around people with AA and afraid to get to know them. These children feared people with AA were contagious or dying. Too young to understand the situation or the disease, young unaffected children may be less inclined to interact with children with AA." This is why alopecia awareness is so important.

Though I hope to live in a world where everyone is aware and educated about alopecia, it is somewhat difficult to see it through. More people are becoming knowledgeable about alopecia through social media, but it is still difficult for *everyone* to know what it is. I know I don't personally know all of the diseases or conditions other people maybe be facing, so I understand I will always come in contact with somebody who does not know or understand what alopecia is.

The most important thing, however, is *respect*. Teaching kids at a young age everyone is beautiful and unique is crucial. You don't have to be buddies with everyone you meet, yet respecting someone and not judging them based on their appearance before you come to any conclusions speaks volumes. *Don't judge a book by its cover.* I know it's cliché, but someone's personality is what makes them who they are, not their looks.

Being bald does not change or hinder the chances individuals have to achieve their dreams. I've met many alopecians along the way, and they have accomplished great things. Whether it be within their community, school, or on TV or social media, they did not let alopecia affect what they could achieve and showed everyone else around them they could do anything. I was blessed with the opportunity to speak with Nico, Kylie, Kevin, Deeann, and Anthony. I have gained so much insight listening to their journeys. They are only a few of the 147 million people with alopecia in the world. They have made differences in numerous lives, no matter how big or small. They changed the frame and continue to do so. Whether it is from a newfound sense of confidence or the increased spread of awareness about alopecia, more alopecians are ready and able to tell their story. We learn to be ourselves because that is most important. Being true to yourself allows you to exude positivity others will be forced to notice.

17

ONE HECK OF A ROLLERCOASTER

————

I love rollercoasters. The adrenaline combined with the wind in your hair or your nice, shiny head on a hot summer day cannot be beat. If you've ever had the opportunity to ride a rollercoaster, you know the feeling. Being free is boundless.

When my family or friends have the chance, we try to make it to the amusement park at least once during the summer. One hot summer day in July 2015, we headed over to Six Flags Great Adventure. Once we went through security and entered the park, we headed straight for Nitro—hands down the best rollercoaster there. Then, my sister wanted to ride the Dark Knight. We thought it was a kiddie ride, but little did we know, it wasn't. We lined up and waited for the ride, and for those of you who aren't familiar with this particular ride, it has many sudden turns. I was still wearing a hat at the time, being extremely insecure about my appearance and going out in public bald. As we were on the ride, I was enjoying myself and not holding on to my hat. Three turns into the ride, my hat flew off and there was no way of getting it back. Luckily, I had a bandanna wrapped on my head. As you very well know by now, I was insecure, and I covered as much baldness as possible. Baseball caps typically have the "hole" or opening in the back so I wrapped my head in a bandanna so no one was able to see any part of my bare head.

After losing my hat on the ride, I was so aware of everything around me. Even with the bandanna, I felt naked. I felt like everyone's eyes were on me. I was constantly scanning the area around me and was not able to really enjoy the moment. All I could think about was if people were staring. I was definitely overthinking it, but I was preoccupied about what others thought of me and could not find the time to have fun. I wanted to leave; however, I was with my friend and family and did not want to be a buzzkill.

Life is full of *ups* and *downs*—just like a rollercoaster. We will all face some type of hardship in one way or another. The hardship may force us to reevaluate ourselves. We might not think it's fair. We will often ask the question, "Why do bad things happen to good people?" Or "Why me?" Yet, regardless, every single one of us will have our personal strength tested.

I grew up in a Christian church and I asked God why *I* had to go through this. Why did it have to be me with alopecia? I was already a socially awkward child, somewhat overweight, and had low self-esteem. I had so many questions throughout my journey. *Why did it have to me?* For months after I was diagnosed, I felt so unlucky. I was frustrated with myself and the guy upstairs. My family was such a strong support system, but I couldn't vent or share my feelings with them. They wouldn't be unbiased toward my feelings. I tried my best to express my feelings; nevertheless, they would end up getting frustrated or annoyed with me. Maybe they were frustrated with themselves and did not know how to help me. So why did it have to be me? I now know the answer.

I now view alopecia as a gift. It wasn't so easy to accept that in the beginning and throughout my journey. But I do believe I was given this gift to show others with courage and confidence, you can surmount your hurdles. However, that courage and confidence was not easy to obtain either. I was fortunate to have such a strong support system and people around me who accepted me for me. Without those people, I honestly feel I would have lived a lifetime of sadness. I surrounded myself with the right people and was able to find my confidence.

I hope I can be there for my fellow alopecians and be a person they can talk to. I hope to inspire others, and with this book, I can share my story and the stories of many others. I am fortunate to have such an amazing support system that allowed me to be comfortable in my own skin and enabled me to embrace my baldness and be myself. I want to create a positive and lasting impact on others' lives, which is also a reason why I'm working toward becoming a nurse in the near future.

For you alopecians out there, whatever you may believe in, just know the universe chose *you*. Actually, this is for everyone who is going through their own set of struggles; you should know the universe chose you. *You.* It chose you because *you* are the one who can show others surmounting any type of hardship allows you to come out stronger. There will be many ups and downs, but you are chosen to get up when you're down and fly even higher when you're up.

Overcoming a hardship is never easy. I was moved to tears when watching the 2020 film *I Still Believe,* starring KJ Apa and Britt Robertson. This movie is based on a true story that walks us through the life of Jeremy Camp, a Christian music star, and his journey of love with the love of his life, Melissa Lynn Henning-Camp, who was diagnosed with ovarian cancer shortly before they were married. Britt Robertson's character, Melissa Camp, says something that really stood out to me: "If one person's life is changed by what I go through, it will be all worth it." This really resonated with me because I constantly asked myself why I had to get alopecia, but if the universe chose me to share my journey and I am able to help at least *one* person realize their true beauty and self-worth, even though it was one heck of a rollercoaster ride, *it will be all worth it.*

ACKNOWLEDGMENTS

———

During the process of creating this book, I had the amazing opportunity to interview many individuals who shared inspirational stories and offered motivational advice. Special thanks to Anthony Carrigan, Kylie Bamberger, Kevin Bull, Chloe Bean, Shalice Ader, Deeann Callis Graham, Julianne Chandler, Nicolas Srut, Dr. Angela Rodgers, and Dr. Leslie Castelo-Soccio.

Thank you to all my friends and family who support me. Thank you to my peers and faculty from Marlboro Middle School, Marlboro High School, and Rutgers University who continue to motivate me. Thank you to my coworkers who always brighten my day.

Lastly, thank you to New Degree Press, especially the individuals who turned this dream into a reality. *Massive* thanks to Eric Koester, Lyn S., Brian Bies, Trisha Giramma, Jack Cohen, Kat Li; the video editing team, Bianca daSilva, Erika Arroyo, Solaja Slobodan, and Gjorgji Pejkovski; and the cover design team.

Thank you to all the people listed below who contributed to my campaign. It means the world. Your name in the acknowledgments section does not justify how much you mean to me. I wholeheartedly appreciate every single one of you and I cannot thank everyone enough.

Abby Vasquez
Alex Mikhaylov
Alexander Ahn
Alexis Papavero
Alyssa Giordani
Amanda Palombo
Andrew Lau
Angela Lee
Annamaria
Saraceni
April Huie
Ariana Materia
The Lin Family
Beverly Yu
The Tse Family
Chainwen Chu
Chioma Ibeku
Christian Pittari
Christine Chung
Christine Tang
Christopher
Cousillas
Christy Lee
Cindy Poon
Connie lau
Connie Pun
Cozy Apuzzo
The Chin Family

Danielle
Valentino
Dave Ryden
Dawn Moore
Debbie Costanzo
Diana Hom
Diana Peng
Elaine Baho
Elaine Vuong
Ellie Rosenberg
Elsiea Chin
Emily Young
Emmy P. Yee So
Eric Koester
Erin Nam
Erin Rooy
Esther Wong
Flora Fung
Florence Kan
Gabriel Carter
Gabriel Lyons
George Henson
Gianna
Bellantuono
Virginia
McDonald
Gisella Romeo
Grace Cheng
Grace Hou

Helen Pityinger
Hector Mena
Hope Grindlinger
Horraine Lai
Izen Su
Jacob Miller
Jason Lu
Jenn Angelone
Jenn Sun
Jenna Lombardi
Jennifer Vozzo
Jessica Marshall
Jessica Shaw
Jessica Zheng
Jimmy & Sherry
Yuen
Joann Fremgen
Jonas Labermeier
Judy Chen
Julie Mauritzen
Julie Pfeffer
Kaleigh Wargo
Kamy Chung
Kara Chin
Karli Rogers
Kasidy Sisson
Katherine Caruso
Katina Tsakiris
Kayla Fittipaldi

Kelsey Dowd
Kendall Ripetta
Kenneth K. Long
Kit Bing Yick
Kristen Vaccher
Kyle D. Warren
Lila Ginsburg
Lorraine Smith
Louisa Chuah
Lucia Xie
Maengel Tolentino
Malcolm Ting
Man Chan
Maria Baker
Maria Sholty
Marina Fortuna
Marissa Hazel
Mary Chen
Max Eleftherio
May Ho
Megan Kim
Melissa Spirn
Melodie Young
Michael Bodnar
Michelle Fleischer

Mira Yin
Mohana
Chakrabarti
Nancy Uy-Chu
Nicole Fopeano
Paige Roberts
Patricia Rachlis
Peter Kujawski
Peter Peng
Robert Tarloff
Robyn Harrington
Rocco Tomazic
Ron Romeo
Ryan Bochinski
Ryan Chu
Ryan Geran
Sage Savoia-Di
Gregorio
Sarah Posen
Shumei Kuo
So Ping Hung
Stephanie Li
Stephanie Mullin
Sue L. Lau
Susan Cheung

Suzie Tam
Talia Rosen
Tara Reich
Teri Collins
Theresa Besso
Thomas Edralin
Tiffany Yuen
Tim McConnell
TJ Bryant
Tommy Kaiser
Tommy Yuen
Tracey Licciardi
Trivik Ragha
Tuan (Jake)
Nguyen
Vaicy Sit
Victoria Samour
Wai Yuen
Wanda Ng
Winnie Huang
Winnie & Ashley
Young
Yiwen Chu
Yves Brouard

APPENDIX

INTRODUCTION

National Alopecia Areata Foundation. "FAQ's." Accessed January 8, 2021. https://www.naaf.org/faqs.

THE DISCOVERY

Asad, Usman, Daniel Wallis, and Michelle Tarbox. "Ophiasis Alopecia Areata Treated with Microneedling." *Proceedings; Baylor University Medical Center* vol. 33, no. 3 (2020): 413-414. DOI:10.1080/08998280.2020.1753456.

Gupta, M. A., A. K. Gupta, and G. N. Wattell. "Stress and Alopecia Areata: A Psychodermatologic Study." *Acta Dermato-Venereologica* vol.77, no. 4 (1997): 296–298. DOI: 10.2340/0001555577296298.

National Alopecia Areata Foundation. "FAQ's." Accessed January 8, 2021. https://www.naaf.org/faqs.

THE DECISION

Hunt, Nigel and Sue McHale. "The Psychological Impact of Alopecia." *BMJ* 331, no. 7522 (October 2005): 951-953. DOI: https://doi.org/10.1136/bmj.331.7522.951.

Nerenz, D.R., R.R. Love, H. Leventhal, and D.V. Easterling. "Psychosocial Consequences of Cancer Chemotherapy for Elderly Patients." *Health Services Research: U.S. National Library of Medicine* 20, no. 6 Pt 2 (February 1986): 961–976. https://www.europepmc.org/article/PMC/1068916.

Wolf, Naomi. *The Beauty Myth: How Images of Beauty Are Used Against Women.* London: Vintage, 1991.

STEREOTYPICAL AND SOCIAL STIGMAS

Hall, Kristin. "The Psychological Impact of Male Hair Loss." *Hair Loss* (blog). *Hims*, June 7, 2019.

Hunt, Nigel and Sue McHale. "The Psychological Impact of Alopecia." *BMJ* 331, no. 7522 (October 2005): 951-953. DOI: https://doi.org/10.1136/bmj.331.7522.951.

Stough, Dow, Kurt Stenn, Robert Haber, William M. Parsley, James E. Vogel, David A. Whiting, and Ken Washenik. "Psychological Effect, Pathophysiology, and Management of Androgenetic Alopecia in Men." *Mayo Clinic Proceedings* 80, no. 10 (2005): 1316-1322. DOI: https://doi.org/10.4065/80.10.1316.

BROW GAME: WEAK TO FLEEK

Venugopal, Manila. "Can Wearing Makeup Boost Cognition as Well as Confidence?" *News 18*, July 30, 2017. https://www.news18.com/news/lifestyle/health-and-fitness-can-wearing-makeup-boost-cognition-as-well-as-confidence-1478279.html.

MASKS ON

Thompson, Karl. "What Is Normal?" *ReviseSociology*, September 3, 2018. https://revisesociology.com/2018/09/03/what-is-normal/.

CONQUERING MY FEAR OF DATING

Love, Alopecia (blog). "Bald Girl in the Dating World." February 10, 2017. Accessed August 27, 2021. https://lovealopecia.wordpress.com/2017/02/10/bald-girl-in-the-dating-world/.

JOKE'S ON YOU!

Rafique, Rafia. and Nigel Hunt. "Experiences and Coping Behaviours of Adolescents in Pakistan with Alopecia Areata: An Interpretative Phenomenological Analysis." *International Journal of Qualitative Studies on Health and Well-Being* 10, no.1 (2015) e26039. DOI: https://doi.org/10.3402/qhw.v10.26039.

Wilkins, Julia and Amy J. Eisenbraun. "Humor Theories and the Physiological Benefits of Laughter." *Holistic Nursing Practice* 23, no.6 (2009): 349-352. DOI: 10.1097/HNP.0b013e3181bf37ad.

THE NEW GENERATION OF ALOPECIANS

Day, Harvey. "How We're All Being Changed by Influencer Culture." *BBC*, February 16, 2019. https://www.bbc.co.uk/bbcthree/article/b5488f38-e9c4-4e0c-95e2-3002f47f88f8.

Tankovska, H. "Number of Social Media Users Worldwide from 2017 to 2025." *Statista*, published July 2020. https://www.statista.com/statistics/278414/number-of-worldwide-social-network-users/.

CHANGING THE FRAME

Aschenbeck, Kelly A., Sarah L. McFarland, Maria K. Hordinsky, Bruce R. Lindgren, and Ronda S. Farah. "Importance of Group Therapeutic Support for Family Members of Children with Alopecia Areata: A Cross-Sectional Survey Study." *Pediatric Dermatology* 34, no.4 (2017): 427–432. DOI: https://doi-org.proxy.libraries.rutgers.edu/10.1111/pde.13176.

Hankinson, Andrew, Heidi McMillan, and Jeffery Miller. "Attitudes and Perceptions of School-Aged Children Toward Alopecia Areata" *JAMA Dermatol* 149, no. 7 (July 2013): 877–879. DOI: 10.1001/jamadermatol.2013.601.

The Hill. "Ayanna Pressley Applauded for House Speech on Alopecia Areata." September 22, 2020. Video, 5:15. https://www.youtube.com/watch?v=l4U14yMQCtk.

ONE HECK OF A ROLLERCOASTER RIDE

Erwin, Andrew and Jon Erwin. *I Still Believe.* March 2019; Mobile, Alabama: Kingdom Story Company Kevin Downes